THE
GOLFER'S
LOGBOOK

PETER ALLISS
THE
GOLFER'S
LOGBOOK

Collins
Grafton Street, London
1984

William Collins Sons and Co Ltd
London Glasgow Sydney Auckland
Toronto Johannesburg

British Cataloguing in Publication Data
Alliss, Peter
The golfer's logbook.
1. Golf
I. Title II. James, Julian
796.352 GV965
ISBN 0 00 217332 8

First published in Great Britain 1984
Copyright © Peter Alliss and Julian James 1984

Made by Lennard Books
Mackerye End
Harpenden, Herts AL5 5DR

Editor Michael Leitch
Designed by David Pocknell's Company Ltd
Production Reynolds Clark Associates Ltd
Printed and bound in Yugoslavia by
Mladinska Knjiga, Ljubljana

The Golfer's Logbook
was devised by Julian James

Acknowledgments
Cover photograph by Peter Campion
The golf equipment used in the cover photograph
was provided by Dunlop Sports Golf Division
Photographs reproduced in the book were provided by
Phil Sheldon

Contents

Introduction

Over the years I have been to many houses and hotels where it has been the tradition to keep a Log or Game Book in which all the events connected with a particular sport are faithfully recorded. I am not myself a 'sporty' type in the huntin'-shootin'-fishin' sense, but I have had endless pleasure just browsing through these books and reading accounts of the various days, what the weather was like, who was there, what and how many they caught, and so on.

Memories of such days can be a source of enormous pleasure to all who are involved. It is strange that the idea of a Logbook has not previously made an impression on the golf world, but I am sure this present venture will not remain unique for long.

The *Golfer's Logbook* is the inspiration of Julian James, headmaster of St Aubyns Preparatory School, Rottingdean. In 1979 Julian, a member of the Royal and Ancient and the Golf House Club, Elie, introduced his three sons Christopher, then aged 12, David (10) and Andrew (3) to golf when they were on holiday at Elie. As he himself says:

'It was when my already untidy desk became littered with more and more notes recording the boys' progress – the first shot of ten yards, the first hole in less than 30 – that I remembered having a Game Book as a child and went to St Andrews to look for a golfing equivalent. To my surprise, none could be found, so I thought it would be fun to make up my own.'

Julian produced a working model, and this, with some small modifications and extra pages of 'editorial' entertainment, is very much what you now see before you. Most of the detailed work of filling in the pages is self-explanatory, and we have included a few lines of introduction here and there, along with some well-known and less-familiar golfing quotes, as a reminder of the spirit in which the book was conceived.

Not everyone is a Samuel Pepys, and the idea of keeping a fairly large diary may be unfamiliar to some readers. All I would really wish to do here is to offer you my best wishes and say: 'Be bold – and be honest.'

This is your own book of memories. We hope it is something you will look back on with lasting pleasure – and no twinges of conscience because what you have set down is not quite the unvarnished truth. You missed that last putt, remember? It should say 70 at the bottom there, not 69. Remember, too, the more thoroughly you fill in the pages with your details and observations, the better it will be – both for yourself and for anyone else you may allow to leaf through it.

Some of the Game Books I have seen are almost works of art. They achieve this level partly through style – because the author has developed a personal way of describing events crisply and, very often, with humour – and partly through presentation. This also is worth a few minutes' thought. Do you remember how marvellous something as mundane as an old-fashioned ledger could look if it was beautifully set out in the same copperplate hand, using the same type of nib throughout, and the same colour of ink?

Plan your *Golfer's Logbook* by asking yourself how you would like it to look when it is finished. Should you use black ink or blue? Are you going to write with a 'real' pen? Are you going to buy a sheet of blotting paper (almost a dying industry these days)? We don't want any blots or splodges, please. But, whether you use a quill or a gold biro, take your time when you fill in the columns. Think ahead, far ahead. Years from now, someone will pick up this book and in it will find the definitive account of your golfing achievements and your memories of those days. Now that, surely, is worth more than a little bit of care and attention.

Or maybe you have different ideas. You would really prefer to use the *Logbook* as a kind of scribbler's pad which is for your eyes only. That is entirely your affair. In this brief Introduction I am merely airing a few ideas and options which perhaps had not occurred to everyone. What is, however, common to all is the opportunity to recapture in this book your feats and personal impressions of this extraordinary game.

— T H E —
GOLFER'S
LOGBOOK

—— NAME ——

—— ADDRESS ——

—— TELEPHONE ——

—— GOLF CLUB ——

Personal Record

Sir, or Madam, This Is Your Golfing Life! A place to delve into the deep past – those days when you held your first driver, putted your first putt, played shots that will always hold a place in your repertoire of favourite daydreams.

FIRST LESSON

FROM   DATE

CLUB/COURSE

FIRST ROUND OF GOLF

COURSE   DATE

PLAYED WITH

FIRST SET OF CLUBS

WOODS   DATE

IRONS/PUTTER

PURCHASED FROM

FIRST MEMBERSHIP

CLUB   DATE

PROPOSED BY

SECONDED BY

FIRST HANDICAP

HANDICAP   DATE

CLUB

FIRST COMPETITION WIN

COMPETITION   DATE

CLUB

PRIZE

MASHIE   NIBLICK   IRON   DR

———— BEST GROSS SCORE (18 HOLES) ————

SCORE _____ DATE _____

COURSE _____ SSS _____

———— BEST NETT SCORE (18 HOLES) ————

GROSS SCORE _____ HANDICAP _____

NETT SCORE _____ DATE _____

COURSE _____ SSS _____

———— OTHER MEMORABLE OCCASIONS ————

_____

_____

_____

_____

_____

_____

_____

_____

_____

_____

_____

_____

_____

_____

_____

_____

_____

_____

_____

_____

_____

_____

Home Club Details

Be your own club historian, and set down what you really feel about each of those holes you play so regularly. Record the holes that give you the most trouble. Why is it always the 13th that you come to grief on? Not everyone is tormented by it; could it possibly be that you are playing the hole wrongly? Put it all down on these pages – the facts *and* the opinions. You will learn a little bit more about yourself, and how to play the course, and the benefits will come tumbling in.

CLUB

ADDRESS

TELEPHONE   FOUNDED

CAPTAIN

SECRETARY   TELEPHONE

PROFESSIONAL   TELEPHONE

ASSISTANTS

CLUB HISTORY
FAMOUS MEMBERS & GREAT CHARACTERS

MAJOR COMPETITIONS HELD ON THE COURSE

COURSE RECORD

AMATEUR	SCORE	PROFESSIONAL	SCORE

THE GOLFER'S LOGBOOK

COURSE DETAILS
(IF MORE THAN ONE COURSE ENTER DETAILS IN 'OTHER COURSES' SECTION)

HOLE No	TEES SSS			TEES SSS			COMMENTS
	YARDS/METRES	PAR	SI	YARDS/METRES	PAR	SI	
1							
2							
3							
4							
5							
6							
7							
8							
9							
OUT							
10							
11							
12							
13							
14							
15							
16							
17							
18							
IN							
OUT							
TOTAL							

My Favourite Courses

The index of British Clubs and Courses listed in that invaluable guide, the *Golfer's Handbook*, runs to 2,126 entries. The choice of where to play is little short of bewildering, and for that reason we shall limit our coverage in this section to mainland Britain; there will be no little forays abroad, however tempting (but see also the section on 'Holiday Golf').

The sheer number of courses brings home to me another interesting point, which is that I have not been to, let alone played, nearly as many courses in Britain as people tend to assume. Partly this is because I did not have an amateur career. I was one of the first of the modern generation of golfers who join the professional tour while they are still young (too young, some might say), and this does limit the number of courses they can expect to see because the tour tends to go round to the same places each year for the understandable reason that these courses are geared to the big events and have the best facilities.

Sadly the days of the amateur tour are buried and gone, but in the prime of people like Joe Carr and Michael Bonallack a good player with just a little money behind him — not much, you could live for a week on a fiver — had a wonderful opportunity to roam the country and play in scores of amateur tournaments, certainly one a week and maybe two or three. My own best means of extending my knowledge of British golf courses was to play in exhibition matches, which I enjoyed even though the travelling hither and thither got rather frantic at times. Fortunately, too, I have been able to spend my whole life under the influence of golf, and so have had the time to form a considered view of what I like best in British golf courses.

The family background must always be a leading factor. Provided you have enjoyed the environment in which you grew up, you are bound to stay fond of it in later life. I know that my favourite type of golf course will always feature the heather, pine, gorse and silver birch that I first met at Ferndown, near Bournemouth, where my father was the professional. Later I spent a further thirteen happy years as professional at nearby Parkstone, overlooking Poole Harbour.

There is a special warmth that goes with those courses, whether they are on the south coast or in some oasis further north. I like my golf courses to be pretty much the same all through the year, and it is one of the great advantages of heather and pine that it is so unchanging. Even in winter, when you are wearing seventeen sweaters, the pine trees are

always green, and the only real changes you notice are when
the gorse breaks out in yellow flowers, the heather turns
into a purple carpet and you may come across a
splendid patch of rhododendrons in bloom.

That is my very favourite type of British
golf course. Another type with much to commend
it is the downland course. These abound along the
Sussex coast, at Worthing and above Brighton, and
in the Cotswolds. There, on a fine clear day, you
are confronted with the most beautiful long-
range views and conditions for golf are
marvellous. On the other hand, when anything
stronger than a mild zephyr is blowing, even
the faintest drizzle has a habit of turning into
a raging hurricane and raindrops that were
falling lightly against your cheeks suddenly
turn into machine-gun bullets. Allied to the
more difficult terrain, with long
climbs up the valleys and over
the hilltops, these conditions
can prove strenuous.

Not as strenuous, though, as our third group, the great seaside links courses where the Open championships have been contested since 1860 (if you count the first eleven years when Willie Park, the Morrises and other early giants fought for The Belt). Those really are spectacular courses and there is nothing like them anywhere else in the world. A day spent in good company at Muirfield, or Turnberry — which is one of my favourites — or Hoylake, Lytham and St Annes, Birkdale, Carnoustie, St Andrews, Royal St George's, is a true delight. All the same, much as I enjoy going there for the great tournaments, they are not my ideal fare for everyday golf, which is our main concern here.

The 2nd green at Royal Birkdale

Heather and Pine

Going back to my Dorset roots, I must say that the area around Bournemouth and Poole is blessed with some wonderful golf courses. Along with Ferndown and Parkstone, there's the Broadstone Golf Club, the Isle of Purbeck, Knighton Heath (the old Northbourne club), Meyrick Park and Queen's Park — two fine municipal courses — and

Brockenhurst, a little further away in the New Forest. All are thoroughly attractive and pleasant for a day's golf.

There are many other nests of heather and pine. On the Berkshire–Surrey border, near Ascot, for instance, is the Berkshire Golf Club, with its Red and Blue courses; nearby is Sunningdale with three courses, the Old, the New, and Sunningdale Ladies; and Wentworth, where the East and West courses await you. In this affluent part of the world the profusion of fine golf courses is both impressive and reassuring: Hankley Common, West Hill, Woking, Worplesdon, New Zealand, West Surrey . . . Just north of the Thames, near Slough, is the Stoke Poges club, where Sean Connery filmed a famous golf sequence for the James Bond film *Goldfinger*. Sometimes, in choosing a course, one is swayed by the memory of having played some good golf there. I know I am. Still, never mind. It's all part of your golfing memories.

Further north, this same type of course can be found at Woburn in Bedfordshire, at Woodbridge in Suffolk, King's Lynn in Norfolk, and over the Wash at Woodhall Spa in Lincolnshire. They have them too in the Leeds area: at Moortown, Alwoodley, and Moor Allerton – the only British course designed by Robert Trent Jones, and where I spent ten enjoyable years. In the new metropolitan county of Tyne and Wear a good example is the Northumberland Golf Club, where the fairways wind their way through Newcastle race course. Near the great city of Birmingham, the Little Aston course has lovely turf, silver birch and pine, and is one of my all-time favourites. In the same area are Whittington Barracks and Beau Desert.

In Scotland, go east of Edinburgh and take your pick of the Gullane, Muirfield, Dunbar and North Berwick courses. The Edinburgh courses themselves are well worth a visit. Try Barnton (Royal Burgess) or Bruntsfield where I played in the Boy's Championship, way back in 1946. As you move north, the big attractions are the seaside links courses: St Andrews, the home of golf, and Carnoustie, arguably the most difficult of all the championship courses (though sadly a little in decline since it was taken off the championship rota). Closer to Aberdeen, go inland a bit, and you will come upon fine courses such as Edzell, Aboyne and Banchory. Further north is Nairn, and way up near the top you will find Royal Dornoch which, I confess, I have not yet had the privilege of visiting, although the reports of it are excellent.

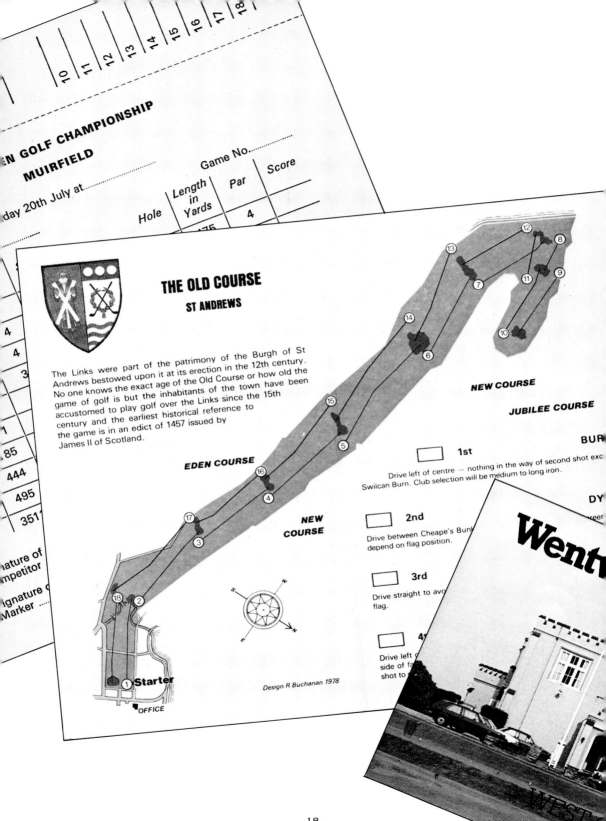

GOLF CHAMPIONSHIP

MUIRFIELD

day 20th July at

Hole	Length in Yards	Par	Score	Game No.
		4		

THE OLD COURSE
ST ANDREWS

The Links were part of the patrimony of the Burgh of St Andrews bestowed upon it at its erection in the 12th century. No one knows the exact age of the Old Course or how old the game of golf is but the inhabitants of the town have been accustomed to play golf over the Links since the 15th century and the earliest historical reference to the game is in an edict of 1457 issued by James II of Scotland.

EDEN COURSE

NEW COURSE

NEW COURSE

JUBILEE COURSE

BUR

DY

reer

Design R Buchanan 1978

Starter

OFFICE

1st
Drive left of centre — nothing in the way of second shot exc
Swilcan Burn. Club selection will be medium to long iron.

2nd
Drive between Cheape's Bun
depend on flag position.

3rd
Drive straight to avo
flag.

4
Drive left
side of fa
shot to

Went

WEST

4
4
3

1
85
444
495
351

nature of
mpetitor

ignature
Marker

Downland Magic

Time, now, to look at the delights – and occasional terrors – of downland golf. Worthing is one of my special favourites. My memories of that course go back to 1949, when I played there in one of my first competitions and won the prize for long driving. I also remember Tom Haliburton setting the world record there – 126 for 36 holes.

At Worthing, you stride along magnificent valleys, scale hills and meet old members who will point out the chalk walkways where pilgrims travelled on the long road from Winchester to Canterbury – eight hundred years ago. While you sit up there on the Downs, waiting for those slowcoaches in front to get out of the way, a great slice of ancient history stands revealed, and you find yourself wondering about the old monks tottering along the paths and through the forest, coping with villains and vagabonds who'd strip them to their sandals . . . When your thoughts return to golf, you look around you and try to trace the tees and flags and see where you still have to go. Over there is a huge mound with a green on top. 'Good heavens!' you think, 'we'll never get up there. Should we send for a taxi?'

There are no great names among the golf courses that are set just back from the sea in the South Downs, but from Bognor Regis to Bexhill (Highwoods) you will find a number of fine rolling courses with dramatic views over some of our finest countryside. Perhaps it is because so many of the towns are holiday resorts that I associate those courses with splendid days-out, enjoyed in the kind of leisurely way you find all too rarely nowadays. No-one is in a hurry to look at their watch and say 'We're closed'; stewards never need to put their feet up, and the teas are superb – with beautifully cut sandwiches and anchovy toast (one of my special favourites), all washed down with bottomless pots of strong hot tea.

This pattern is happily repeated in Gloucestershire and the Cotswolds. There aren't all that many courses in these parts, but Gloucestershire has always produced a formidable bunch of county golfers. This may well be because they learned early to play into the wind, and off difficult slopes, so that by the time they had mastered their hilly domain they had become very respectable players.

I remember taking part in many an exhibition match in the Cotswolds for the Lord Roberts Workshops and Forces Help Society. Cirencester is a particularly pleasant course – only just over 6,000 yards in length, but very sporty and enjoyable. Cotswold Hills is longer (6,716 yards) and from the back tees is a considerable test. At Minchinhampton there are two courses – the Old and the New – and both are to be reckoned with; Stinchcombe Hill is another I thoroughly recommend for a good day out. It's not a long course, in fact the Standard Scratch Score is only 68, but you will enjoy coming to grips with it. As ever in this neck of the woods, the views are simply magnificent.

And Down to the Sea

Very few of our great seaside courses are so located that you can actually see the sea while you are playing. At Turnberry you can, and that is what makes it potentially the most spectacular course in the UK. At Lytham and St Annes there is no view of the water, nor is there at Hoylake or Birkdale. At Carnoustie you don't really see the sea; at Royal St George's you only glimpse it on a couple of holes.

Royal Porthcawl is something of an exception because there you can look across to the sea from virtually all points on the course. Situated right on the shore, midway between Cardiff and Swansea, this is a very handsome golf course, which also has particularly happy associations for the Alliss family because it was at Porthcawl that my father began his golfing career.

However, as I mentioned before, classical seaside vistas of rocks and sand and crashing waves are all very well, but they are often accompanied by raging winds and blinding storms and are not the friendliest places to be. If our main objective here is to recommend pleasant courses where the golf is played for fun, we will do better to focus on the small courses, preferably arranged in two loops of nine or, in an ideal world, three loops of six, so that you are never a million miles from the clubhouse, you never feel isolated, and there is always a friendly shelter nearby that you can hide under until the rainclouds have passed.

This is not at all what you will find at Turnberry, where it's nine holes and two and a half miles out, and much the same coming back. Unless you are a hardened nature-lover, passionate about nesting cormorants or all-night badger watches, you may think to yourself: 'Suppose it rains when I'm out there?' And spend so much time thinking about how to insulate your body from the angry gods with waterproofs, boots and umbrellas that the golf becomes secondary.

Or you may be lucky. You may strike a balmy evening when you can stride along in your shirt sleeves, getting in a quick nine holes before dinner. No-one else is around, just you, your partner and the wheeling gulls; the sea is calm, the sun beginning to set. Magnificent.

And yet it is probably wiser to end on a more domestic note. How about Hayling Island? That is a delightful course, often bypassed by people whizzing from Southampton to Chichester or Brighton.

Another gem which gave me a lot of pleasure is Littlestone. Just away from the sea near Romney Marsh, and therefore not in the most fashionable location, I found it a most attractive course with a pleasant clubhouse. Here too they seemed to understand perfectly one's wants, which include a smile and a friendly welcome, and, after the golf, a good tea with hard-boiled eggs, hot toast, and don't spare the fruit cake. I hope it hasn't changed.

Courses to Play

One of the greatest pleasures of the game is to be able to play challenging courses in such a variety of beautiful settings up and down the country. Another marvel is that you are able to stand where the greats have stood. Not many can say that about the Centre Court at Wimbledon, or the centre circle at Wembley, or the cricket square at Lord's. But golf is different: you *can* march where the gods have marched, and that surely is one of the great delights of the game. On this page is a countrywide selection of courses that you might like to try if you find yourself in the neighbourhood. We have also left space for you to key in others that you have played and enjoyed.

1	St Andrews	21	Woburn	41	
2	Gleneagles	22	Moor Park	42	
3	Royal Dornoch	23	Berkshire	43	
4	Nairn	24	Sunningdale	44	
5	Royal Aberdeen	25	Wentworth	45	
6	Rosemount	26	Walton Heath	46	
7	Muirfield	27	Royal St George's	47	
8	Kilmarnock, Barassie	28	Royal Cinque Ports, Deal	48	
9	Turnberry	29	Worthing	49	
10	Brancepeth Castle	30	Hayling	50	
11	Royal Lytham and St Annes	31	Ferndown	51	
12	Royal Birkdale	32	Parkstone	52	
13	Formby	33	St Mellion	53	
14	Alwoodley	34	Trevose	54	
15	Woodhall Spa	35	Saunton	55	
16	Little Aston	36	St Pierre	56	
17	Frilford Heath	37	Royal Porthcawl	57	
18	King's Lynn	38	Portmarnock	58	
19	Hunstanton	39	Killarney	59	
20	Woodbridge	40	Ballybunion	60	

COURSES TO PLAY   COURSES PLAYED

Rounds Played

Here we reach the nitty-gritty — the pages where you chart in full and faithful detail your own or your team's performance in each round. Remember to keep your scorecard in a safe place so you can write all this up at home without having to trust to memory. Remember, too, that if you are playing in a competition you will have to hand in your scorecard after the round — and you will *never* see it again. So jot down the information on a duplicate card. In matchplay, where your actual score per hole is not the most essential factor, you may still find it worthwhile keeping a record of the holes on which you played well. It all makes good reading later!

ROUND NO	COURSE											SSS				DATE		

PLAYING WITH

PLAYING AGAINST

COMPETITION   WEATHER

TEES PLAYED OFF   TIME

HOLE NO	1	2	3	4	5	6	7	8	9	10	11	12	13	14	15	16	17	18
PAR																		
SELF																		
OPPONENT																		
RESULT																		

TOTAL	OUT	IN	GROSS	HANDICAP	NETT

MATCH/COMPETITION RESULT

COMMENTS

ROUND NO	COURSE											SSS				DATE		

PLAYING WITH

PLAYING AGAINST

COMPETITION   WEATHER

TEES PLAYED OFF   TIME

HOLE NO	1	2	3	4	5	6	7	8	9	10	11	12	13	14	15	16	17	18
PAR																		
SELF																		
OPPONENT																		
RESULT																		

TOTAL	OUT	IN	GROSS	HANDICAP	NETT

MATCH/COMPETITION RESULT

COMMENTS

P.A. Vale, a great man of letters, wrote: 'Style is a fetish with many players. The man who worries about his style ought to give up golf.'

ROUND NO	COURSE												SSS			DATE		
PLAYING WITH																		
PLAYING AGAINST																		
COMPETITION							WEATHER											
TEES PLAYED OFF							TIME											
HOLE NO	1	2	3	4	5	6	7	8	9	10	11	12	13	14	15	16	17	18
PAR																		
SELF																		
OPPONENT																		
RESULT																		
TOTAL	OUT		IN			GROSS				HANDICAP				NETT				
MATCH/COMPETITION RESULT																		
COMMENTS																		

ROUND NO	COURSE												SSS			DATE		
PLAYING WITH																		
PLAYING AGAINST																		
COMPETITION							WEATHER											
TEES PLAYED OFF							TIME											
HOLE NO	1	2	3	4	5	6	7	8	9	10	11	12	13	14	15	16	17	18
PAR																		
SELF																		
OPPONENT																		
RESULT																		
TOTAL	OUT		IN			GROSS				HANDICAP				NETT				
MATCH/COMPETITION RESULT																		
COMMENTS																		

'One must wait out the coming round of the club. Keeping the head down will not always do this. Keeping the mind on the impact is of more importance.' *So said H.B. Martin.*

ROUND NO	COURSE										SSS				DATE		

PLAYING WITH

PLAYING AGAINST

COMPETITION   WEATHER

TEES PLAYED OFF   TIME

HOLE NO	1	2	3	4	5	6	7	8	9	10	11	12	13	14	15	16	17	18
PAR																		
SELF																		
OPPONENT																		
RESULT																		

TOTAL	OUT	IN	GROSS	HANDICAP	NETT

MATCH/COMPETITION RESULT

COMMENTS

ROUND NO	COURSE										SSS				DATE		

PLAYING WITH

PLAYING AGAINST

COMPETITION   WEATHER

TEES PLAYED OFF   TIME

HOLE NO	1	2	3	4	5	6	7	8	9	10	11	12	13	14	15	16	17	18
PAR																		
SELF																		
OPPONENT																		
RESULT																		

TOTAL	OUT	IN	GROSS	HANDICAP	NETT

MATCH/COMPETITION RESULT

COMMENTS

Harold Hilton, a great amateur who won the Open in 1892 and 1897 and designed a club for my father: 'I am a believer in the use of heavy wooden clubs provided they are within control of the player's physical powers.' That's interesting because I always used clubs which many people thought were very heavy.

ROUND NO	COURSE													SSS		DATE	
PLAYING WITH																	
PLAYING AGAINST																	
COMPETITION								WEATHER									
TEES PLAYED OFF							TIME										

HOLE NO	1	2	3	4	5	6	7	8	9	10	11	12	13	14	15	16	17	18
PAR																		
SELF																		
OPPONENT																		
RESULT																		

TOTAL	OUT		IN			GROSS			HANDICAP			NETT		

MATCH/COMPETITION RESULT

COMMENTS

ROUND NO	COURSE													SSS		DATE	
PLAYING WITH																	
PLAYING AGAINST																	
COMPETITION								WEATHER									
TEES PLAYED OFF							TIME										

HOLE NO	1	2	3	4	5	6	7	8	9	10	11	12	13	14	15	16	17	18
PAR																		
SELF																		
OPPONENT																		
RESULT																		

TOTAL	OUT		IN			GROSS			HANDICAP			NETT		

MATCH/COMPETITION RESULT

COMMENTS

George Greenwood: 'Golf is the most skilful of all games. It has baffled mankind for centuries, and because of its inherent subtleties will continue to do so for all time.'

ROUND NO	COURSE										SSS				DATE		
PLAYING WITH																	
PLAYING AGAINST																	
COMPETITION							WEATHER										
TEES PLAYED OFF							TIME										
HOLE NO	1	2	3	4	5	6	7	8	9	10	11	12	13	14	15	16	17	18
PAR																		
SELF																		
OPPONENT																		
RESULT																		
TOTAL	OUT		IN			GROSS				HANDICAP				NETT			
MATCH/COMPETITION RESULT																	
COMMENTS																	

ROUND NO	COURSE										SSS				DATE		
PLAYING WITH																	
PLAYING AGAINST																	
COMPETITION							WEATHER										
TEES PLAYED OFF							TIME										
HOLE NO	1	2	3	4	5	6	7	8	9	10	11	12	13	14	15	16	17	18
PAR																		
SELF																		
OPPONENT																		
RESULT																		
TOTAL	OUT		IN			GROSS				HANDICAP				NETT			
MATCH/COMPETITION RESULT																	
COMMENTS																	

Etiquette on the Course

It should all be very simple and plain to see. But it never is. The matter of etiquette on the course regularly sparks off the most extraordinary rows and nonsense. Most of these incidents could be avoided; all are a pain in the neck.

It should be as straightforward as learning to drive a car. If you want a licence, you have to know what it says in the Highway Code. And unless your ambitions are distinctly bent or anti-social, or you have been watching too many car-chase movies on television, you will be happy to follow these rules of the road because you know that they exist to protect the safety and well-being of *all* road-users, not just your good self.

Back to golf, and we might begin with appearances. It is not asking a lot that golfers should turn up at the clubhouse looking neat and tidy. And yet there is always a steady stream of famous, not-so-famous and even infamous characters who arrive for a round of golf looking like tramps. Why they do it I do not know. It certainly can't help either their self-image or the opinions that others are bound to form of them. Perhaps the dreaded term 'inverted snobbery' has some place here; I am not sure. What I am quite certain of is that a person's appearance will be reflected in his or her play. If they are neat and tidy to look at, there is a more than good chance that they will have a proper respect for the rules and be a pleasure to go round with. A scruff, on the other hand, will be not only a visual disgrace, but a menace and an embarrassment to his playing partners *and* to the people following immediately behind.

One of the remarkable things about golfing behaviour is that it is actually easier to play a neat and tidy game. For instance, if your ball goes off-line, do you a) watch and mark where it goes, or b) shut your eyes? If the answer is (b), you probably throw clubs and swear a lot into the bargain. Enough said, I think, on that particular aspect of play.

However, on the grounds that no-one is perfect, and that we all need to have our memories jogged from time to time, here is a small refresher course on some general points of golfing etiquette:

Always be ready to play Don't imitate the professionals you see on television, with all their extraordinary mannerisms – don't be like the men or women who play their chip shots from the edge of the green to within six inches of the hole; then push their trolley to the other side of the green; solemnly take off the glove; the ball is then marked; the six-inch putt, when at last it is made, is only holed because the glove has now been transferred to its ritual site sticking out of the back pocket. All this hoo-ha adds more and more minutes to the time it takes to complete a round of golf. This now averages about four hours, which is totally ridiculous.

Make sure you know the number on your ball A simple enough point to remember, but how much easier life becomes when you arrive in the rough and find two balls looking up at you. (Alternatively, put a mark on your ball with a biro.)

Park your trolley properly When you come up to the green, have a look to see where the next tee is and place your trolley on that side.

Be kind to the putting surface Don't scuff your feet about on the putting surface like a bull preparing to charge. When you take out the flag, try not to spear it into the ground but lay it down gently on its side.

Marking the ball There is a simple drill for this. Your marker is always placed *behind* the ball, and the order of events is always: 'Disc down, ball up'. Then, when you are ready to play, it is: 'Ball down, disc away'.

Divots We have all heard that we should replace our divots on the fairway. But really this should only be done when it is reasonable to do so. There is no point in replacing a little patch of grass if it has no hope of growing. There is a school of thought which reckons that only about five per cent of replaced divots ever take again. On short holes, in particular, it should not be necessary to replace divots. Far better if they are collected once or twice a week by the groundstaff, and the damage repaired with a little sand, soil and seed. The reason is that if you stand on a loose divot, it can easily move under your foot. You slip, and a bad shot is your reward for someone else's good intentions.

Be a good neighbour Always try to keep play moving on the course. If you are in trouble at a short-hole green, for instance, stand aside and let the people on the tee play up, and then you can putt out while they are walking along. Try not to be too loud or obtrusive – this is rather like playing your transistor in the garden and not sparing a thought for the people in the surrounding houses and gardens.

Be fair-minded If you are playing to winter rules which allow you to place your ball within six inches, remember that you can only place it once. If you pop it on top of a convenient wormcast and it rolls off – too bad. The essence of golf is that you should be prepared to take the rough with the smooth. Expect to win some, by all means, but expect to lose some as well. Too many people are obsessed with what the Americans call 'having the edge'. In the professionals' world this is more understandable, but at club level it is an attitude which can erode the whole spirit in which the game is played.

That example, and the whys and wherefores of placing the ball, has many many parallels which you are bound to encounter every so often. How you then deal with these situations depends very much on your attitude of mind. Is the ball on the fairway or not? Are you one of those players who automatically decides that, because it is *his* ball, it must be three-quarters on the fairway and only one-quarter off it? Do you sometimes need a kind friend to point out that the ball is actually three-quarters *off* the fairway, and so does not qualify to be placed under the winter rules for cut grass?

Golf continually brings people face to face with such lines of demarcation. How they decide to behave is of course up to them, but there is no doubting that, on each and every occasion, on one side of the line are truth and fairness. The other side of the line is the territory of the cheat.

THE GOLFER'S LOGBOOK

Rounds Played

ROUND NO	COURSE												SSS			DATE		

PLAYING WITH

PLAYING AGAINST

COMPETITION   WEATHER

TEES PLAYED OFF   TIME

HOLE NO	1	2	3	4	5	6	7	8	9	10	11	12	13	14	15	16	17	18
PAR																		
SELF																		
OPPONENT																		
RESULT																		
TOTAL	OUT		IN			GROSS			HANDICAP				NETT					

MATCH/COMPETITION RESULT

COMMENTS

ROUND NO	COURSE												SSS			DATE		

PLAYING WITH

PLAYING AGAINST

COMPETITION   WEATHER

TEES PLAYED OFF   TIME

HOLE NO	1	2	3	4	5	6	7	8	9	10	11	12	13	14	15	16	17	18
PAR																		
SELF																		
OPPONENT																		
RESULT																		
TOTAL	OUT		IN			GROSS			HANDICAP				NETT					

MATCH/COMPETITION RESULT

COMMENTS

Bobby Jones: 'Good form in golf means efficiency — the art of expending upon the ball all the energy of the swing without wastage.'

ROUND NO	COURSE													SSS			DATE	
PLAYING WITH																		
PLAYING AGAINST																		
COMPETITION								WEATHER										
TEES PLAYED OFF								TIME										

HOLE NO	1	2	3	4	5	6	7	8	9	10	11	12	13	14	15	16	17	18
PAR																		
SELF																		
OPPONENT																		
RESULT																		

TOTAL	OUT		IN			GROSS			HANDICAP				NETT		

MATCH/COMPETITION RESULT

COMMENTS

ROUND NO	COURSE													SSS			DATE	
PLAYING WITH																		
PLAYING AGAINST																		
COMPETITION								WEATHER										
TEES PLAYED OFF								TIME										

HOLE NO	1	2	3	4	5	6	7	8	9	10	11	12	13	14	15	16	17	18
PAR																		
SELF																		
OPPONENT																		
RESULT																		

TOTAL	OUT		IN			GROSS			HANDICAP				NETT		

MATCH/COMPETITION RESULT

COMMENTS

Ted Ray: 'Never waste time and temper attempting to play the unplayable.'

ROUND NO	COURSE											SSS				DATE		
PLAYING WITH																		
PLAYING AGAINST																		
COMPETITION							WEATHER											
TEES PLAYED OFF							TIME											
HOLE NO	1	2	3	4	5	6	7	8	9	10	11	12	13	14	15	16	17	18
PAR																		
SELF																		
OPPONENT																		
RESULT																		
TOTAL	OUT		IN				GROSS			HANDICAP				NETT				
MATCH/COMPETITION RESULT																		
COMMENTS																		

ROUND NO	COURSE											SSS				DATE		
PLAYING WITH																		
PLAYING AGAINST																		
COMPETITION							WEATHER											
TEES PLAYED OFF							TIME											
HOLE NO	1	2	3	4	5	6	7	8	9	10	11	12	13	14	15	16	17	18
PAR																		
SELF																		
OPPONENT																		
RESULT																		
TOTAL	OUT		IN				GROSS			HANDICAP				NETT				
MATCH/COMPETITION RESULT																		
COMMENTS																		

William Wilson: 'Every golfer should aim at irreproachable green manners. Speaking plainly, he should do nothing to annoy his opponent. Self-confidence and concentration are the first essentials of a fine game. Neither can be possessed if your mind is divided between wishing your opponent ill and your own play.'

ROUND NO	COURSE											SSS			DATE		

PLAYING WITH

PLAYING AGAINST

COMPETITION   WEATHER

TEES PLAYED OFF   TIME

HOLE NO	1	2	3	4	5	6	7	8	9	10	11	12	13	14	15	16	17	18
PAR																		
SELF																		
OPPONENT																		
RESULT																		

TOTAL	OUT		IN			GROSS			HANDICAP			NETT		

MATCH/COMPETITION RESULT

COMMENTS

ROUND NO	COURSE											SSS			DATE		

PLAYING WITH

PLAYING AGAINST

COMPETITION   WEATHER

TEES PLAYED OFF   TIME

HOLE NO	1	2	3	4	5	6	7	8	9	10	11	12	13	14	15	16	17	18
PAR																		
SELF																		
OPPONENT																		
RESULT																		

TOTAL	OUT		IN			GROSS			HANDICAP			NETT		

MATCH/COMPETITION RESULT

COMMENTS

Francis Ouimet, surprise winner of the American Open Championship in 1913, after tying with Vardon and Ray: 'I believe that the great golfers think of three things when they play any old kind of shot, namely relaxation, slow backswing and keeping the eye on the ball.'

ROUND NO	COURSE										SSS				DATE		

PLAYING WITH

PLAYING AGAINST

COMPETITION						WEATHER											

TEES PLAYED OFF						TIME											

HOLE NO	1	2	3	4	5	6	7	8	9	10	11	12	13	14	15	16	17	18
PAR																		
SELF																		
OPPONENT																		
RESULT																		

TOTAL	OUT		IN			GROSS			HANDICAP				NETT		

MATCH/COMPETITION RESULT

COMMENTS

ROUND NO	COURSE										SSS				DATE		

PLAYING WITH

PLAYING AGAINST

COMPETITION						WEATHER											

TEES PLAYED OFF						TIME											

HOLE NO	1	2	3	4	5	6	7	8	9	10	11	12	13	14	15	16	17	18
PAR																		
SELF																		
OPPONENT																		
RESULT																		

TOTAL	OUT		IN			GROSS			HANDICAP				NETT		

MATCH/COMPETITION RESULT

COMMENTS

Difficult Short Holes

In my experience the most interesting and challenging short holes have been exactly that – short holes. Over the years it has become the fashion, particularly on American courses, to design short holes to just under the maximum length. The result is that when there is a little bit of breeze against, even the top professionals have to use a driver. When you are trying to hit a green no bigger than two king-size sheets, that is very difficult indeed.

To me the great delight of short holes is that they should be both short, perhaps barely over 100 yards, and yet very testing. One of my favourites is the 7th at Pebble Beach, on the Monterey Peninsula in the United States. It is 110 yards or so from the top of the hill to the green which sits out in the ocean. The green is tiny and surrounded by bunkers; over the back, sea otters lie out on the rocks banging abalones on their tummies and laughing at your efforts.

I have played that hole with a 2-iron, and I have also played it with a sand-iron, just trying to flip it up and hoping the wind will carry it through the air and land it on that little green carpet, so near and yet so far from where you stand on the tee. The tales of disaster wrought by that little hole are vastly out of proportion to its size. I have heard of very respectable players taking twelve shots, while others have holed in one.

In that same neck of the woods is the 16th hole at Cypress Point. This is one of my very favourite courses in the world, and yet, if you designed that course today, most observers would condemn you. They would quickly point out that you followed your short par-three 15th hole with a long short hole – all very unorthodox and perhaps improper, and it has made the 16th extremely difficult to deal with. Only three people have ever holed out in one – and one of them was Bing Crosby who did it about thirty years ago and whose feat is recorded on the honours board in the clubhouse.

Scenically this hole is just as magnificent as the one at Pebble Beach. Below the green are the rocks, the otters and the ocean, and a quarter of a mile out to sea great whales go blasting past en route to their feeding grounds, sending up vast plumes of spray into the air.

Both are classic golf holes. Their settings have obviously made a contribution to their fame, as have the great histories of the two golf clubs, which are barely a couple of miles apart. But what really marks out these holes is the way they were designed. 'Happened' is possibly a better word, because neither was part of the master plan of some eminent golf-course architect. Both were laid out by ordinary members – who had the remarkable good fortune to produce masterpieces.

What they achieved, almost by accident, is rather like a Sunday painter going out one day and coming back with a 'Munnings'. 'What's that?' his friends all say in complete astonishment. 'How did you do that?' 'Well,' he says, 'I just thought I'd go out and find a horse and paint it. Bloody good, isn't it?' 'Yes!' says one of the friends. 'It's marvellous. Could you do another one – for me?' The chap scratches his head. 'No, I don't think I could really.' 'What? Look, don't be silly. Just go out and find another horse. I'll get one in for you, if you like.' 'No,' says the reluctant Master. 'It's not that I don't want to. It's just that this painting kind of came together just right. There was this hill, that lovely tree over there, the horse in the middle . . . it just sort of happened, do you see?'

So it was with the 7th at Pebble Beach, which apparently just sort of happened as a way of getting from the 6th to the 8th. Out to one side was the sea, which placed certain limitations on what could be done. So they looked again at the space available, and filled it with a golf hole that has become one of the most talked-about and admired in the world.

Much closer to home, the 2nd at Wentworth is one that I especially like. Its fascination is not that it is a particularly beautiful or classical short hole, but that so much can happen there. The hole is built up in the air, so if you pitch short the ball can come all of twenty yards back off the green and downhill. Thousands have been in this very spot before you, so your lie might be a little scruffy as you wonder where to go with your second shot, and end by popping it up in the air and praying hard. Alternatively, you might be in the bunker on the right; then there's that great tree, getting bigger every year, it seems to have an annual growth rate far quicker than the average tree. And they've put the pin in the far right-hand corner! Should you play to the front of the green and try and two-putt? If you are a bit strong you may still be lucky and screw back off the bank at the back of the green. Or, if you go a yard too far and stay up at the top, what then? Well, that would mean chipping down to the hole. The pin is near that bunker, but if you are a little too hard you will go off the end and down the hill . . .

On and on goes the debate. That is the wonder of a good short hole. The same possibilities of multiple confusion, of doom and disaster, and just conceivably of triumph, await every arrival at Troon's 8th hole, the justly famous Postage Stamp, at 123 yards the shortest hole in British championship golf. The bunkers surrounding that miniscule green are deep and treacherous, and if you land in there the temptation must be to hit firmly out. But go at it too hard and you will be across the green in less time than it takes Hurricane Higgins to traverse a snooker table, and off the other side into another deep and treacherous bunker. In no time at all your once-promising round of golf has disintegrated into a mortifying trek, back and forth across the 8th green.

'Come on, Charlie!' shouts a voice, 'you've only had seven. Keep going, my son.' 'Oh, Lord,' you think, 'why did I come out today?' You keep going, and eventually you hole out for some monstrous score. 'Bloody silly hole, that was,' you say later to a chap in the bar. 'Do you think so?' he says. 'I got on in one.'

Such is the power of a great short hole to undo the *sangfroid* of all who play it. Other British holes that I would put in the same category are the 11th at St Andrews, the 4th at Turnberry (called 'Woe-be-tide'), the 13th at Muirfield, the 18th at Parkstone and the 1st at Lytham and St Annes. The latter two are special rarities in that you seldom find a course that either opens or finishes with a short hole. Near Ascot, the Berkshire has a collection of beautifully sculptured short holes which are a delight to play – always assuming that you are at the peak of form and fitness, and supremely confident. Or let us hope, at least, that these fine holes will bring out the very best in you.

The 2nd at Wentworth

The 8th (Postage Stamp) at Troon

Rounds Played

ROUND NO	COURSE								SSS		DATE		

PLAYING WITH

PLAYING AGAINST

COMPETITION   WEATHER

TEES PLAYED OFF   TIME

HOLE NO	1	2	3	4	5	6	7	8	9	10	11	12	13	14	15	16	17	18
PAR																		
SELF																		
OPPONENT																		
RESULT																		

TOTAL	OUT		IN			GROSS			HANDICAP			NETT	

MATCH/COMPETITION RESULT

COMMENTS

ROUND NO	COURSE								SSS		DATE		

PLAYING WITH

PLAYING AGAINST

COMPETITION   WEATHER

TEES PLAYED OFF   TIME

HOLE NO	1	2	3	4	5	6	7	8	9	10	11	12	13	14	15	16	17	18
PAR																		
SELF																		
OPPONENT																		
RESULT																		

TOTAL	OUT		IN			GROSS			HANDICAP			NETT	

MATCH/COMPETITION RESULT

COMMENTS

Bobby Jones said: 'Without doubt a very considerable percentage of high handicap players, mentally if not physically, actually begin a hitting effort immediately from the top of the backswing.'

ROUND NO	COURSE										SSS				DATE		

PLAYING WITH

PLAYING AGAINST

COMPETITION   WEATHER

TEES PLAYED OFF   TIME

HOLE NO	1	2	3	4	5	6	7	8	9	10	11	12	13	14	15	16	17	18
PAR																		
SELF																		
OPPONENT																		
RESULT																		
TOTAL	OUT		IN			GROSS			HANDICAP				NETT				

MATCH/COMPETITION RESULT

COMMENTS

ROUND NO	COURSE										SSS				DATE		

PLAYING WITH

PLAYING AGAINST

COMPETITION   WEATHER

TEES PLAYED OFF   TIME

HOLE NO	1	2	3	4	5	6	7	8	9	10	11	12	13	14	15	16	17	18
PAR																		
SELF																		
OPPONENT																		
RESULT																		
TOTAL	OUT		IN			GROSS			HANDICAP				NETT				

MATCH/COMPETITION RESULT

COMMENTS

THE GOLFER'S LOGBOOK

Grantland Rice: 'No-one can control tension anymore than one can control lightning. Tension must be stopped at the source and the starting place is the brain or mind.'

ROUND NO	COURSE											SSS			DATE		

PLAYING WITH

PLAYING AGAINST

COMPETITION   WEATHER

TEES PLAYED OFF   TIME

HOLE NO	1	2	3	4	5	6	7	8	9	10	11	12	13	14	15	16	17	18
PAR																		
SELF																		
OPPONENT																		
RESULT																		

TOTAL	OUT	IN	GROSS	HANDICAP	NETT

MATCH/COMPETITION RESULT

COMMENTS

ROUND NO	COURSE											SSS			DATE		

PLAYING WITH

PLAYING AGAINST

COMPETITION   WEATHER

TEES PLAYED OFF   TIME

HOLE NO	1	2	3	4	5	6	7	8	9	10	11	12	13	14	15	16	17	18
PAR																		
SELF																		
OPPONENT																		
RESULT																		

TOTAL	OUT	IN	GROSS	HANDICAP	NETT

MATCH/COMPETITION RESULT

COMMENTS

44

H.B. Martin: 'Great golfers may be born and not made but a successful bunker artist learns his art from long and tedious practice.'

ROUND NO	COURSE										SSS				DATE		
PLAYING WITH																	
PLAYING AGAINST																	
COMPETITION							WEATHER										
TEES PLAYED OFF							TIME										
HOLE NO	1	2	3	4	5	6	7	8	9	10	11	12	13	14	15	16	17	18
PAR																		
SELF																		
OPPONENT																		
RESULT																		
TOTAL	OUT		IN			GROSS			HANDICAP				NETT					
MATCH/COMPETITION RESULT																		
COMMENTS																		

ROUND NO	COURSE										SSS				DATE		
PLAYING WITH																	
PLAYING AGAINST																	
COMPETITION							WEATHER										
TEES PLAYED OFF							TIME										
HOLE NO	1	2	3	4	5	6	7	8	9	10	11	12	13	14	15	16	17	18
PAR																		
SELF																		
OPPONENT																		
RESULT																		
TOTAL	OUT		IN			GROSS			HANDICAP				NETT					
MATCH/COMPETITION RESULT																		
COMMENTS																		

J.D. Dunn: 'The first rule of etiquette ought to read: "Wait until you are asked before offering any suggestions".'

ROUND NO	COURSE													SSS		DATE		

PLAYING WITH

PLAYING AGAINST

COMPETITION								WEATHER										

TEES PLAYED OFF								TIME										

HOLE NO	1	2	3	4	5	6	7	8	9	10	11	12	13	14	15	16	17	18
PAR																		
SELF																		
OPPONENT																		
RESULT																		

TOTAL	OUT		IN		GROSS		HANDICAP		NETT	

MATCH/COMPETITION RESULT

COMMENTS

ROUND NO	COURSE													SSS		DATE		

PLAYING WITH

PLAYING AGAINST

COMPETITION								WEATHER										

TEES PLAYED OFF								TIME										

HOLE NO	1	2	3	4	5	6	7	8	9	10	11	12	13	14	15	16	17	18
PAR																		
SELF																		
OPPONENT																		
RESULT																		

TOTAL	OUT		IN		GROSS		HANDICAP		NETT	

MATCH/COMPETITION RESULT

COMMENTS

Oozlers and Plonkers

To gamble or not to gamble? Well, we know it can be a very seductive prospect to compete for a pound or two with your playing partner, and we also know that there is a lot of it about, and that the R & A does not like it, particularly when the stakes creep up and clubs and other organizations run auction sweepstakes and give away lavish 'illegal' prizes. In some respects it is difficult not to appear to sermonize when on the subject of golf and betting.

One of the main rules for club players must be: don't get taken to the cleaners. Remember that people who want to bet heavily are trying to take your money to subsidize their income. You can spot the heavy gambler easily enough because of the jargon.

He might say: 'We'll play five, five and five.' This means you bet five pounds on the first nine holes, five on the second and five on the match. Then he adds: 'With automatic presses.' This gives each player the right to press or increase the stakes. Let us suppose you won the first two holes. Your opponent may then say: 'I will press,' and the stakes go up by an agreed amount, say by fifty per cent. A full press means you double your stake, not just on the first nine holes but on the match as well. So now you are in for another ten pounds. If you continue to win, he may press you again, and then it is beginning to mount up. Your opponent now recovers (miraculously?) to win the first nine, then the second nine and the match. You might have chosen to press him on the back nine, and a game which you thought had started out quite innocently ends up with you losing about a hundred quid – which can come as quite a shock.

I have never been attracted to betting on the golf course, although I know that some of my fellow professionals were more than enthusiastic punters and acquired something of the aura of Damon Runyan characters for their extravagant wins and losses. Henry Cotton had a good remedy for keeping things under control. When he was captain of the first Ryder Cup team in which I played in 1953, he made us all put a pound (or was it ten shillings?) in the kitty, and then we went round the Wentworth course. Everyone had to keep a card, and the overall winner took the pot.

That was fine for us, because it just made us concentrate a little bit harder. In the same way, it can be quite amusing to bet 10p, or even 50p, on a putt or some other aspect of the game. However, beware the

Blade reaches bottom
of arc in front
of Ball

golf hustler, particularly in the United States where the breed has proliferated.

The hustler's first ploy is to tell you that he hasn't played for a long time. Just look at his hands. Assuming he is a right-hander, if his left hand is white and his right hand is nut brown, you know he is telling you stories. No matter how hard he may have worked to preserve a porcelain pallor on his face by hiding under a Sam Snead-type hat, the glove is a dead giveaway. If the left hand is white and the right is brown, you know he has been out there flogging balls and that all his antics on the first tee, as he strives to impress you that he is really a very ordinary player, are just a smokescreen. Beware!

If you don't mind this sort of intrigue, and are quite happy to go in for a heavy flutter now and again, then it is absolutely essential to get all your gaming rules set out and understood by all parties long before you reach the first tee. If you fail in this, you could well be heading for an unpleasant scene later.

That is one of the main things that has always deterred me from betting: the knowledge that it can go sour, whereas, if the stake was simply a round of drinks, all that extra, unnecessary needle would be avoided. For needle there certainly can be. If you are playing for fifty pounds or more, it suddenly becomes very important to know whether your ball is on this line or that line, and whether you can move it. In a sense, you have almost ceased to play golf as it was intended to be played; now the main thought in your head has nothing to do with your golf technique. It is: 'Gawd! This is for *fifty quid*!'

I really can't see the sense in it. You might do better to toss a coin to see who gets the fifty, and then go and have a decent game of golf. There doesn't seem to me to be a proper connection between playing golf and the business of transferring quite a large sum of money from one person's back pocket to another person's back pocket.

I am not, on the other hand, against those silly little bets that people indulge in just for a laugh – and for which the stakes are correspondingly tiny. I am talking now of the oozlers, plonkers and other daft ploys that you will inevitably hear about if you hang around long enough in the bar rooms which do so much to support our great game. In case you feel yourself rather under-informed in this department, below, in no particular order, is a brief guide to some of the terms and the feats they describe. Always bear in mind that there are many regional variations – so make quite sure that you know what you and your partners are talking about before you lay your precious pence on the line.

Oozler The winner is the player nearest the pin on a short hole. In Dorset, moreover, he must get a three. If he doesn't, then the **reverse oozler** comes into play and the stake money goes to the other side. Alternatively, the oozler may be carried forward without penalty to the next short hole.

Plonker Again, it's the ball nearest the pin on the short hole – but that's all. It doesn't matter about the putts; with plonkers you win or lose with your first shot.

Ferret A chip in from off the green with any club other than a putter.

Golden Ferret Holing from a bunker (*à la* Lee Trevino).

Sandy Getting out of the bunker and holing out with one putt.

Hissing Sid The last player to three-putt on a green.

Woodpecker If you hit your tee shot and moments later hear the bonk! of ball on tree trunk – that's a woodpecker.

Fannies For male members only. Your tee shot is so feeble that it fails to pass the ladies' tee.

Gritter Not getting out of the bunker in one.

Rounds Played

ROUND NO	COURSE										SSS				DATE			

PLAYING WITH

PLAYING AGAINST

COMPETITION　　　　　　　　　　**WEATHER**

TEES PLAYED OFF　　　　　　　　**TIME**

HOLE NO	1	2	3	4	5	6	7	8	9	10	11	12	13	14	15	16	17	18
PAR																		
SELF																		
OPPONENT																		
RESULT																		

TOTAL	OUT	IN	GROSS	HANDICAP	NETT

MATCH/COMPETITION RESULT

COMMENTS

ROUND NO	COURSE										SSS				DATE			

PLAYING WITH

PLAYING AGAINST

COMPETITION　　　　　　　　　　**WEATHER**

TEES PLAYED OFF　　　　　　　　**TIME**

HOLE NO	1	2	3	4	5	6	7	8	9	10	11	12	13	14	15	16	17	18
PAR																		
SELF																		
OPPONENT																		
RESULT																		

TOTAL	OUT	IN	GROSS	HANDICAP	NETT

MATCH/COMPETITION RESULT

COMMENTS

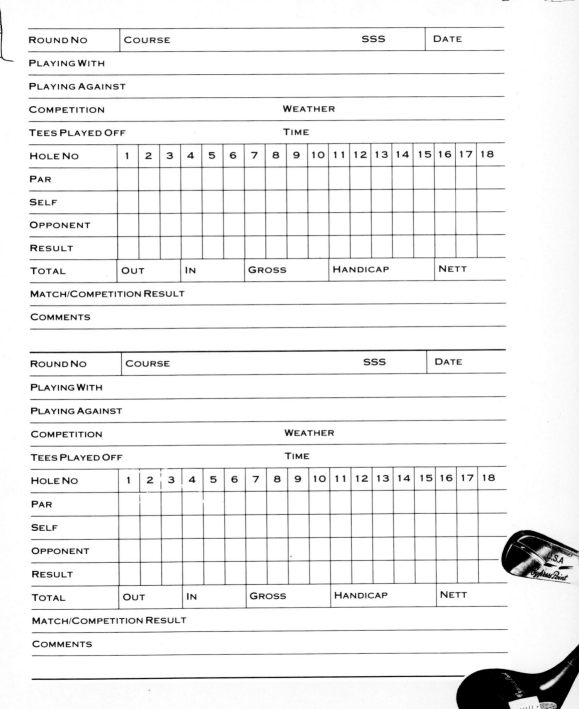

Jack White, once the professional at Sunningdale: 'A cleanly hit but only a moderately hard-hit ball will travel further than a badly hit ball where twice the power has been used.'

ROUND NO	COURSE												SSS			DATE		
PLAYING WITH																		
PLAYING AGAINST																		
COMPETITION								WEATHER										
TEES PLAYED OFF								TIME										
HOLE NO	1	2	3	4	5	6	7	8	9	10	11	12	13	14	15	16	17	18
PAR																		
SELF																		
OPPONENT																		
RESULT																		
TOTAL	OUT		IN			GROSS			HANDICAP				NETT					
MATCH/COMPETITION RESULT																		
COMMENTS																		

ROUND NO	COURSE												SSS			DATE		
PLAYING WITH																		
PLAYING AGAINST																		
COMPETITION								WEATHER										
TEES PLAYED OFF								TIME										
HOLE NO	1	2	3	4	5	6	7	8	9	10	11	12	13	14	15	16	17	18
PAR																		
SELF																		
OPPONENT																		
RESULT																		
TOTAL	OUT		IN			GROSS			HANDICAP				NETT					
MATCH/COMPETITION RESULT																		
COMMENTS																		

Sir Eric Holderness: 'When one sees a ball go off the face of the putter in a timid and irresolute manner, it is clear evidence that the putter is slowing down when it hits.'

ROUND NO	COURSE												SSS			DATE		

PLAYING WITH

PLAYING AGAINST

COMPETITION						WEATHER

TEES PLAYED OFF						TIME

HOLE NO	1	2	3	4	5	6	7	8	9	10	11	12	13	14	15	16	17	18
PAR																		
SELF																		
OPPONENT																		
RESULT																		

TOTAL	OUT		IN			GROSS			HANDICAP			NETT		

MATCH/COMPETITION RESULT

COMMENTS

ROUND NO	COURSE												SSS			DATE		

PLAYING WITH

PLAYING AGAINST

COMPETITION						WEATHER

TEES PLAYED OFF						TIME

HOLE NO	1	2	3	4	5	6	7	8	9	10	11	12	13	14	15	16	17	18
PAR																		
SELF																		
OPPONENT																		
RESULT																		

TOTAL	OUT		IN			GROSS			HANDICAP			NETT		

MATCH/COMPETITION RESULT

COMMENTS

Bobby Jones said: 'No-one ever swings too slowly. Over-effort is the cause of the average golfer's trouble.'

ROUND NO	COURSE											SSS				DATE		
PLAYING WITH																		
PLAYING AGAINST																		
COMPETITION							WEATHER											
TEES PLAYED OFF							TIME											
HOLE NO	1	2	3	4	5	6	7	8	9	10	11	12	13	14	15	16	17	18
PAR																		
SELF																		
OPPONENT																		
RESULT																		
TOTAL	OUT		IN			GROSS			HANDICAP				NETT					
MATCH/COMPETITION RESULT																		
COMMENTS																		

ROUND NO	COURSE											SSS				DATE		
PLAYING WITH																		
PLAYING AGAINST																		
COMPETITION							WEATHER											
TEES PLAYED OFF							TIME											
HOLE NO	1	2	3	4	5	6	7	8	9	10	11	12	13	14	15	16	17	18
PAR																		
SELF																		
OPPONENT																		
RESULT																		
TOTAL	OUT		IN			GROSS			HANDICAP				NETT					
MATCH/COMPETITION RESULT																		
COMMENTS																		

H. Lowe: 'The art of putting consists in hitting the ball with freedom, grace and accuracy right in the middle of the club.'

ROUND NO	COURSE											SSS			DATE		

PLAYING WITH

PLAYING AGAINST

COMPETITION   WEATHER

TEES PLAYED OFF   TIME

HOLE NO	1	2	3	4	5	6	7	8	9	10	11	12	13	14	15	16	17	18
PAR																		
SELF																		
OPPONENT																		
RESULT																		

TOTAL	OUT		IN		GROSS		HANDICAP		NETT	

MATCH/COMPETITION RESULT

COMMENTS

ROUND NO	COURSE											SSS			DATE		

PLAYING WITH

PLAYING AGAINST

COMPETITION   WEATHER

TEES PLAYED OFF   TIME

HOLE NO	1	2	3	4	5	6	7	8	9	10	11	12	13	14	15	16	17	18
PAR																		
SELF																		
OPPONENT																		
RESULT																		

TOTAL	OUT		IN		GROSS		HANDICAP		NETT	

MATCH/COMPETITION RESULT

COMMENTS

Challenging Long Holes

In championship play there are very few holes left that you can call true par-fives. The big boys nowadays aim to reach most par-five greens in two and so get birdies out of them. They really don't like the difficult old-style par-five which is a genuine three-shotter. To listen to some of the pros, you almost get the feeling that they think such holes are unfair, presumably because they are stretched to make par on them.

I think that is an odd, rather selfish view. A par-five is a par-five, and there *should* be something special about it, which cannot simply be overcome by modern big-hitting techniques and balls that go further. It would certainly be a sad day if golf-course architects were to turn their backs on creating genuine par-fives, but the possibility does seem to be there.

I am in favour of the tendency nowadays to make fairways a little bit narrower and more testing, so that greater accuracy is demanded of the club player. At the same time, architects should take care not to hobble the golfer who likes a few holes where he can really smash the ball. That is one of the great primal joys of golf, and woe betide any designer who attempts to suppress it. At club level the big hitter is usually something of a character among his fellow members, and nearly everyone likes to see a few pros out on the course who can really give the ball a spectacular belting.

You find this admiration of the big hitter, the thumper, in other sports. We all loved Bobby Charlton in his day because he came roaring onto those gentle passes which were specially laid on so he could give the ball an almighty crack from all of thirty yards. In cricket, one of the great sights in recent years has been Viv Richards whacking one of his monster drives that went up, up and still further up, and with luck cleared the pavilion altogether.

The 6th at Troon

Length, of course, is not the only factor in judging a good or great par-five. The 6th at Royal Troon is, at 577 yards, the longest hole in British championship golf. Even so, it is relatively straight, and on a calm day the pros will certainly try to get on the green in two – as several did in the 1982 Open. When the wind is against, of course, or gusting from the right, it is a very different story, especially when you are trying to battle through the funnel set by those two critical bunkers, the wide one 80 yards from the green on the left, and the deep one on the right, some 30 yards short of the green.

At Huntingdale Golf Club, in Melbourne, where they play the Australian Masters, there is an enormously long hole of about 620 yards. Even so, if the wind is from behind and the ground good and firm, which it usually is, the Greg Normans of this world can still get on the green with a drive and a 1-iron.

We have so far limited ourselves in this section to long holes that are *bona fide* par-fives. However, on any of our British seaside championship courses a strong wind can convert a hole of some 450 yards into a hugely long and difficult proposition. At Muirfield, the 9th hole is 460 yards, and so a par-four, but, played into the wind, it is one of the most difficult holes in golf. To the left a greystone out-of-bounds wall runs along the entire length of the hole. The fairway bends to the right and narrows to about 15 yards, while in front you can see nothing but acres of rough and a line of gigantic bunkers. Instead of a four, the club player should be thinking in terms of five or five and a half.

At St Andrews there are only two par-fives, but one of these is enough for many players – the dreaded 14th with its enormous Hell Bunker and a string of other traps and pitfalls. First you have to thread a way between the Beardies on the left and the stone wall which angles in from the other side; then if you lay up short of Hell you have to make sure you do not go in the Benty or Kitchen bunkers. Eighty yards past Hell is another cluster, including Grave and Ginger Beer, and then you get to a green which rears up out of a collection of hollows and falls away at the back – all of which may convince you that this is *the* killer hole to beat them all.

Still at the seaside, and in this case almost in the water, we are now standing on the championship tee of the 9th at Turnberry. Here you begin with a hefty blow of some 200 yards across a rocky inlet to a stone cairn marker. Once there, the route to the green is straightforward with no bunkers to interrupt your progress. On this hole the tee shot is all, but with the waves crashing on the shore beneath you, and with the wind against, it all becomes a daunting task.

From the inland courses that I visit regularly, I would select the West Course at Wentworth as a major source of pain and anguish to generations of club golfers. One of these generations, in the years after the Second World War, nicknamed the entire course the 'Burma Road', so it must have kept a few people awake at night during the late Forties. That may be a long time ago, but the degree of hardship in relation to other courses is still pronounced – the difference, to pursue the military metaphor, between serving your time in the Paras rather than the Pay Corps.

The 17th hole is a particularly tough nut. It is 571 yards long, the fairway slopes from left to right with a fierce camber that pushes your ball away from the general direction of the green, there is a dogleg from right to left, out-of-bounds all the way down the left-hand side . . . On paper, curiously, it may not sound quite so evil after all, and another interesting point is that there is not a bunker on this hole. And yet I can assure you, as will many others, including several who competed in the 1984 PGA Championships, that the combination of perils on this hole can make it quite terrifying. It is, in that sense, a *complete* golf hole, facing you with a string of absorbing challenges and never letting you rest for a minute.

The 17th at Wentworth

Rounds Played

ROUND NO	COURSE											SSS			DATE		

PLAYING WITH

PLAYING AGAINST

COMPETITION WEATHER

TEES PLAYED OFF TIME

HOLE NO	1	2	3	4	5	6	7	8	9	10	11	12	13	14	15	16	17	18
PAR																		
SELF																		
OPPONENT																		
RESULT																		
TOTAL	OUT		IN			GROSS			HANDICAP				NETT				

MATCH/COMPETITION RESULT

COMMENTS

ROUND NO	COURSE											SSS			DATE		

PLAYING WITH

PLAYING AGAINST

COMPETITION WEATHER

TEES PLAYED OFF TIME

HOLE NO	1	2	3	4	5	6	7	8	9	10	11	12	13	14	15	16	17	18
PAR																		
SELF																		
OPPONENT																		
RESULT																		
TOTAL	OUT		IN			GROSS			HANDICAP				NETT				

MATCH/COMPETITION RESULT

COMMENTS

Alex Herd: 'There is no coming up one way and coming down another. Your return ticket is only available for the line you went up by.'

ROUND NO	COURSE												SSS			DATE		
PLAYING WITH																		
PLAYING AGAINST																		
COMPETITION							WEATHER											
TEES PLAYED OFF							TIME											

HOLE NO	1	2	3	4	5	6	7	8	9	10	11	12	13	14	15	16	17	18
PAR																		
SELF																		
OPPONENT																		
RESULT																		
TOTAL	OUT		IN			GROSS			HANDICAP			NETT						

MATCH/COMPETITION RESULT

COMMENTS

ROUND NO	COURSE												SSS			DATE		
PLAYING WITH																		
PLAYING AGAINST																		
COMPETITION							WEATHER											
TEES PLAYED OFF							TIME											

HOLE NO	1	2	3	4	5	6	7	8	9	10	11	12	13	14	15	16	17	18
PAR																		
SELF																		
OPPONENT																		
RESULT																		
TOTAL	OUT		IN			GROSS			HANDICAP			NETT						

MATCH/COMPETITION RESULT

COMMENTS

J.W. Beldam: 'Whatever the stance, whatever the grip, whatever the movement the best results are obtained by smoothness and rhythm.'

ROUND NO	COURSE												SSS			DATE		
PLAYING WITH																		
PLAYING AGAINST																		
COMPETITION								WEATHER										
TEES PLAYED OFF								TIME										
HOLE NO	1	2	3	4	5	6	7	8	9	10	11	12	13	14	15	16	17	18
PAR																		
SELF																		
OPPONENT																		
RESULT																		
TOTAL	OUT		IN			GROSS			HANDICAP				NETT					
MATCH/COMPETITION RESULT																		
COMMENTS																		

ROUND NO	COURSE												SSS			DATE		
PLAYING WITH																		
PLAYING AGAINST																		
COMPETITION								WEATHER										
TEES PLAYED OFF								TIME										
HOLE NO	1	2	3	4	5	6	7	8	9	10	11	12	13	14	15	16	17	18
PAR																		
SELF																		
OPPONENT																		
RESULT																		
TOTAL	OUT		IN			GROSS			HANDICAP				NETT					
MATCH/COMPETITION RESULT																		
COMMENTS																		

Harold Hilton: 'There is a great virtue in the gospel of playing your own game and not worrying in respect to what the other fellow is accomplishing.'

ROUND NO	COURSE										SSS				DATE		

PLAYING WITH

PLAYING AGAINST

COMPETITION						WEATHER											

TEES PLAYED OFF						TIME											

HOLE NO	1	2	3	4	5	6	7	8	9	10	11	12	13	14	15	16	17	18
PAR																		
SELF																		
OPPONENT																		
RESULT																		

TOTAL	OUT		IN			GROSS			HANDICAP				NETT		

MATCH/COMPETITION RESULT

COMMENTS

ROUND NO	COURSE										SSS				DATE		

PLAYING WITH

PLAYING AGAINST

COMPETITION						WEATHER											

TEES PLAYED OFF						TIME											

HOLE NO	1	2	3	4	5	6	7	8	9	10	11	12	13	14	15	16	17	18
PAR																		
SELF																		
OPPONENT																		
RESULT																		

TOTAL	OUT		IN			GROSS			HANDICAP				NETT		

MATCH/COMPETITION RESULT

COMMENTS

P.A. Vale: 'If a game is worth playing well it is worth knowing well. And knowing it well cannot mean loving it less.'

ROUND NO	COURSE									SSS					DATE		
PLAYING WITH																	
PLAYING AGAINST																	
COMPETITION							WEATHER										
TEES PLAYED OFF							TIME										
HOLE NO	1	2	3	4	5	6	7	8	9	10	11	12	13	14	15	16	17	18
PAR																		
SELF																		
OPPONENT																		
RESULT																		
TOTAL	OUT		IN			GROSS			HANDICAP				NETT					

MATCH/COMPETITION RESULT

COMMENTS

ROUND NO	COURSE									SSS					DATE		
PLAYING WITH																	
PLAYING AGAINST																	
COMPETITION							WEATHER										
TEES PLAYED OFF							TIME										
HOLE NO	1	2	3	4	5	6	7	8	9	10	11	12	13	14	15	16	17	18
PAR																		
SELF																		
OPPONENT																		
RESULT																		
TOTAL	OUT		IN			GROSS			HANDICAP				NETT					

MATCH/COMPETITION RESULT

COMMENTS

Holiday Golf

The main distinction here is between the family holiday, where the old man nips off and plays a few rounds – and nowadays may be joined by his missus if the kids can look after themselves, or you have hired a statuesque Scandinavian to guard them – and the all-out golfing holiday. Although the latter is much more golf-orientated than the casual business of getting in three or four rounds during your holiday fortnight, the two are not wholly different.

Even if you are just pottering down to a quiet chalet in the West Country, don't think that all you have to do is bung the clubs in the boot and everything else will look after itself. You will be astonished how much better everything is if you take the trouble to arm yourself with a few documents.

Many clubs in Britain let visitors play unaccompanied – but by no means all, especially at weekends. If you are in a holiday area, you are very likely to come upon a crowd of visitors all battling to get on at once and a harassed secretary trying to sort out the ones he approves of from the lunatics who will be out there for six hours, butchering his greens and littering the place with empty bottles, sandwich wrappers and other plastic or rubberized vessels too horrible to contemplate.

This is your chance to shine. Stepping forward with a smile, you introduce yourself and explain that you are down in the area for a few days and would love to play a round on his (the secretary's) extremely fine and beautiful course which you have heard so much about. Without pausing, you now whip out an introductory letter from your club secretary and a photocopy of your handicap certificate. How much more effective this will be than going unprepared and having to stammer: 'Well, I am a member at Wentingdale, I, I, I *really* am . . .' and getting the cold fish-eye stare in return and the fatal verdict: 'I'm very sorry, but we do require some written evidence from our visitors.'

The same principle applies abroad, particularly if you are in one of the less popular golfing countries, in Holland, say, or West Germany, where the golf may be part of a general sports or country club set-up and they will certainly only want you if you look respectable *and* seem to know what you are about. So don't be afraid to dress up a bit. Now is the time to flaunt all your nice bits and pieces, and perhaps even the mink-lined head-covers! But remember: over there they like nothing more than to sit down and flick through your papers, documents of identity, letters of introduction on crested notepaper, signed and sealed and *Alles in Ordnung.* Without them you cannot be friends.

But why be awkward? It's really no great sweat to prepare and carry a few bits of paper around with you, especially if this is going to lead to your having a far more interesting and better holiday. It's a little like carrying your driving licence and insurance certificate with you. If you are stopped by the police, you may be able to deal with the incident there and then, provided you have the proper papers. If you don't, you have all the bother of digging them out at home, sending them off within four days – with an accompanying letter, of course, and did you remember to take a copy for your files? No? Oh, well, if it hasn't been posted yet, perhaps you ought to steam open the envelope and take the letter down to that shop with the Xerox and get it photocopied before you post it. If you take a roll of Sellotape with you, and a stamp, you can seal the envelope straight away . . .

And on and on until well past tea-time. Anyway, point made – I hope. Go organized.

I have mentioned a couple of countries in Northern Europe, and this is a good point at which to raise the important question of *where* to go for a good golfing holiday. We do not have space here to start a worldwide survey of golf courses, but enough people are now coming back from the Costa del Sol and saying what murder it was to get a round of golf at all, that it does seem to be time to consider where they should go next.

There is little doubt that the courses of Southern Spain are thoroughly swamped for ten months a year. Next door, however, in Portugal, there are some very fine golf courses along the Algarve which are not too crowded – yet. Still in Southern Europe, Italy has some good courses, mainly in the northern part of the country (try Garlenda, near Alassio). Greece has a few, including a good one on Corfu, and there is a good scattering all the way through France. For me, though, the best golf in France is just across the Channel, at Le Touquet and Hardelot-Plage, which is less than ten miles from Boulogne and a delightful course. So, if you have the good fortune to live within striking distance of a hover or ferry service, give these two a go.

Further north, there are some beautiful courses in Belgium, Holland, West Germany, Switzerland and the Scandinavian countries. These, in my view, are where the future lies for golfing holidays. People say that the exchange rates in some of these countries are crippling – and so they may seem compared with the good old days when for years you got twelve DM and twelve Swiss francs to the pound, not the measly three-odd that they give you nowadays. However, people forget that these countries have had very low inflation compared with ourselves, and so the actual value you get has hardly changed at all.

If you are interested, try looking up some of the foreign clubs listed in the *Golfer's Handbook*. You will find that the fees aren't really so bad at all. Equipment, on the other hand, does tend to cost more abroad, so it is worth putting a couple of extra clubs in your bag and taking two or three dozen golf balls with you. The money you save by good housekeeping can either be spent on some other part of your holiday – or why not splurge it on a caddy and really enjoy yourself?

Another point: be flexible about your playing times. In July and August, even those slightly out-of-the-way courses can be crowded, but if you are prepared to make the effort and avoid the rush hours, it is surprisingly easy to get on. Everyone's first thought is to begin play at nine-thirty or ten in the morning – mainly so they can get back in good time for a drink before lunch. Lunch, in the British way of thinking, is an inviolable event and cannot be missed. But when you are on holiday, what does it matter? Try having a good late breakfast and start your round at twelve or twelve-thirty. Very few people want to be on the first tee at midday and you should have no trouble in starting. If your tummy always rumbles loudly when it doesn't receive food between one and one-thirty, take a sandwich with you. End of problem. Just don't chuck the wrapper in the bushes, that's all.

   If you are worried about the heat, don't be. Slap on a good dose of oil or cream when you go out, not forgetting a sensible sun hat. Unless it is exceptionally hot, with no breeze at all, which is rare on most golf courses, you should be all right. Later on, as you are beginning to tire, the afternoon sun will be less fierce and you can finish your round in good heart.
   Nowadays there are all sorts of packages for those who want to try a golf holiday further afield. One of the reasons why the Costa del Sol became so popular as to be almost out of control is that you can leave Manchester or London and be in your hotel in four and a half or five hours. Florida, on the other hand, is a full day's travel away, plus a degree of jet-lag if you are sensitive to it. All the same, if you have a fortnight to spare, there are some attractive holidays around. TWA, for instance, do a trip to Phoenix, Arizona, which, taken in January or February, is a marvellous tonic. You are out in the desert during the daytime, under blue skies; even if you start out with one sweater, that will probably come off about ten o'clock. In the evening it is log-fire time and you will need a couple of sweaters, but altogether it is a most enjoyable place to be at that time of year.

Closer to home, Ireland would be paradise if it wasn't for a slight uncertainty about the weather. The glorious countryside, the uncluttered roads, the warm welcome and the delightful turn of phrase are seductive indeed, as are the many very fine golf courses. I love going there, and will continue to do so, hopefully for many years.

Another variation is to try the West Country off-season. Cornwall in March is a delight. There are umpteen golf courses, all on sand and nice and dry — no typical English mud. The weather can be a bit of a lottery, of course, but down there they are about two months ahead of the rest of the country. Arrive there in the middle of March and the daffodils will have flowered and gone. Trevose, St Enodoc, Lelant — here we come!

With all holiday golf, no matter where you go, the most important secret of all is to maintain everyone's interest. There may be the odd golf nut in your party who thinks it is sacrilege to be anywhere other than out on the course, and who would play 72 holes a day if his legs would support him. Most people, fortunately, are not quite so single-minded, and the trick is to get them to agree that you are going mainly for the break, and hope to play a fair bit of golf while you are away.

This leaves you room to vary the programme. One day, you may only play nine holes in the morning, then have a snooker tournament in the afternoon, and maybe six holes before dinner. Or you might go on an outing somewhere, just like other holidaymakers. It's not a crime. It's more of a crime to batter your way round all the local golf courses twice a day for the sake of it, then to stay up all night playing cards or sitting around in an ill-lit disco in the vain hope that some young girl will find you strangely interesting, and then at the end of it to arrive home feeling thoroughly exhausted and ill.

'Why?' someone asks you. 'What went wrong?'

'Ugh,' you groan. 'I don't know. It may have been because I haven't slept for thirteen nights, or because we all drank a bottle of tequila every hour. Or it may have been all that golf. You can have too much of a good thing, you know.'

'Yes. I do know,' comes the reply. 'I went with you last year.'

Rounds Played

ROUND NO	COURSE								SSS		DATE						

PLAYING WITH

PLAYING AGAINST

COMPETITION   WEATHER

TEES PLAYED OFF   TIME

HOLE NO	1	2	3	4	5	6	7	8	9	10	11	12	13	14	15	16	17	18
PAR																		
SELF																		
OPPONENT																		
RESULT																		

TOTAL	OUT	IN	GROSS	HANDICAP	NETT

MATCH/COMPETITION RESULT

COMMENTS

ROUND NO	COURSE								SSS		DATE						

PLAYING WITH

PLAYING AGAINST

COMPETITION   WEATHER

TEES PLAYED OFF   TIME

HOLE NO	1	2	3	4	5	6	7	8	9	10	11	12	13	14	15	16	17	18
PAR																		
SELF																		
OPPONENT																		
RESULT																		

TOTAL	OUT	IN	GROSS	HANDICAP	NETT

MATCH/COMPETITION RESULT

COMMENTS

John Jacobs said: 'When you are trying to play into the wind, don't hit it harder, hit it better.'

ROUND NO	COURSE									SSS					DATE		
PLAYING WITH																	
PLAYING AGAINST																	
COMPETITION							WEATHER										
TEES PLAYED OFF							TIME										
HOLE NO	1	2	3	4	5	6	7	8	9	10	11	12	13	14	15	16	17	18
PAR																		
SELF																		
OPPONENT																		
RESULT																		
TOTAL	OUT		IN			GROSS			HANDICAP			NETT						
MATCH/COMPETITION RESULT																		
COMMENTS																		

ROUND NO	COURSE									SSS					DATE		
PLAYING WITH																	
PLAYING AGAINST																	
COMPETITION							WEATHER										
TEES PLAYED OFF							TIME										
HOLE NO	1	2	3	4	5	6	7	8	9	10	11	12	13	14	15	16	17	18
PAR																		
SELF																		
OPPONENT																		
RESULT																		
TOTAL	OUT		IN			GROSS			HANDICAP			NETT						
MATCH/COMPETITION RESULT																		
COMMENTS																		

Grantland Rice: 'Put the main control where it belongs, into the hands, wrists and arms. Keep the body as relaxed as possible and give the idea a chance.'

ROUND NO	COURSE									SSS				DATE			

PLAYING WITH

PLAYING AGAINST

COMPETITION	WEATHER

TEES PLAYED OFF	TIME

HOLE NO	1	2	3	4	5	6	7	8	9	10	11	12	13	14	15	16	17	18
PAR																		
SELF																		
OPPONENT																		
RESULT																		
TOTAL	OUT		IN			GROSS			HANDICAP				NETT					

MATCH/COMPETITION RESULT

COMMENTS

ROUND NO	COURSE									SSS				DATE			

PLAYING WITH

PLAYING AGAINST

COMPETITION	WEATHER

TEES PLAYED OFF	TIME

HOLE NO	1	2	3	4	5	6	7	8	9	10	11	12	13	14	15	16	17	18
PAR																		
SELF																		
OPPONENT																		
RESULT																		
TOTAL	OUT		IN			GROSS			HANDICAP				NETT					

MATCH/COMPETITION RESULT

COMMENTS

Seymour Dunn: 'The finished golfer takes his time sizing up his shot, not his stroke, and when he has done this he goes right up and hits the ball.'

ROUND NO	COURSE												SSS			DATE		

PLAYING WITH

PLAYING AGAINST

COMPETITION · WEATHER

TEES PLAYED OFF · TIME

HOLE NO	1	2	3	4	5	6	7	8	9	10	11	12	13	14	15	16	17	18
PAR																		
SELF																		
OPPONENT																		
RESULT																		

TOTAL · OUT · IN · GROSS · HANDICAP · NETT

MATCH/COMPETITION RESULT

COMMENTS

ROUND NO	COURSE												SSS			DATE		

PLAYING WITH

PLAYING AGAINST

COMPETITION · WEATHER

TEES PLAYED OFF · TIME

HOLE NO	1	2	3	4	5	6	7	8	9	10	11	12	13	14	15	16	17	18
PAR																		
SELF																		
OPPONENT																		
RESULT																		

TOTAL · OUT · IN · GROSS · HANDICAP · NETT

MATCH/COMPETITION RESULT

COMMENTS

The great Willie Park Junior, on putting: 'The club should only hit the ball, not the ball and the ground. Even after the ball has been hit, the club should not touch the ground.'

ROUND No	COURSE													SSS			DATE	

PLAYING WITH

PLAYING AGAINST

COMPETITION									WEATHER									

TEES PLAYED OFF									TIME									

HOLE No	1	2	3	4	5	6	7	8	9	10	11	12	13	14	15	16	17	18
PAR																		
SELF																		
OPPONENT																		
RESULT																		

TOTAL	OUT		IN			GROSS				HANDICAP					NETT			

MATCH/COMPETITION RESULT

COMMENTS

ROUND No	COURSE													SSS			DATE	

PLAYING WITH

PLAYING AGAINST

COMPETITION									WEATHER									

TEES PLAYED OFF									TIME									

HOLE No	1	2	3	4	5	6	7	8	9	10	11	12	13	14	15	16	17	18
PAR																		
SELF																		
OPPONENT																		
RESULT																		

TOTAL	OUT		IN			GROSS				HANDICAP					NETT			

MATCH/COMPETITION RESULT

COMMENTS

Great Par-Fours

The classical par-fours are difficult at the best of times. For the handicap golfer, they become impossible when there is a little bit of wind against, because he cannot then reach the green in two. Once you remove the possibility of landing on the putting surface in two shots, the hole in effect becomes a four-and-a-half or a five.

Even the championship player is up against it in such conditions. The distance may be around the 440- or 450-yard mark, and the Nicklauses and Watsons will need a driver and a 3-iron, or a driver and a 4-iron – which is big hitting. Then there are the hazards, which poker-faced architects have placed smack where you don't want them: a big tree, bunkers, a dog-leg, a tricky green, perhaps built into a hill with a little stream running round the back . . . This combination of distance-plus-artfulness produces a formidable test.

Looking first around the British championship courses, I would certainly name the 18th at Royal Lytham and St Annes as one of the great finishing holes. Although it is a mere 389 yards, from the back tee the view can be intimidating. Three or four bunkers march out in echelon down the left, and on the right are two others. Although the ones on the right are shorter, all conspire to channel you into a narrow neck. Some years ago it was possibly worse, for there used to be great banks of gorse over on the right, in the middle of which stood the club flagpole. This made the general effect even more claustrophobic as you stood on the tee, desperately needing your four to finish, because there was nowhere to go except the one obvious, but highly perilous, place between the bunkers. No matter how much mental wriggling you might try on yourself, eventually you *had* to stand up there and drive, and drive well, all of which made it a magnificent hole.

Another daunting place to finish is Muirfield. The fairway is quite wide to begin with, but bunkers on the right (at 190 yards) and on the left (at 210 and 250 yards) push you inwards to aim at a point where the fairway narrows and then stays narrow. A good drive somewhere level with the left-hand bunkers leaves you with a second shot of about 180 yards to the green. But if you lay up short with your first, you are leaving yourself a very difficult task because the front of the green is stoutly guarded by two bunkers, and you will be doing extremely well if you can carry them. Then the green rises up and away from you. An excellent hole.

On the Old Course at Sunningdale the 5th and 6th command special respect, and the 6th in particular because a strip of heather runs up the fairway and effectively puts the brake on all drives. The surface there is rutted and inhospitable, so, regardless of conditions or who you are, you can only go so far with your first shot. Then you have a shot of at least 170 yards to the green. In all weathers, the 6th at Sunningdale is a thinking man's hole.

The 6th at Sunningdale

Still at Sunningdale, we come to the 11th. The green is driveable, but a lot can happen on the way. The drive is blind, for one thing, over a big stretch of heather with a bunker in the hillside and a post that you aim over. To the right is a stand of fir trees and you know that the green is tucked just behind them. So you think: 'If I start one left and get a bit of a cut on it, it will skim round that corner and run up beautifully.' If, though, you don't get that little bit of cut you veer left across the face of the green, where a bunker lurks, and heather, and a bank on the other side . . . This, again, is not a long hole, but it certainly makes you think hard.

Other courses not on the tournament circuit, and therefore seldom seen on television, have some wonderful par-four holes. Swinley Forest, the Berkshire and New Zealand all have a great array of testing holes about 380-460 yards long, with beautifully positioned bunkers and other features that have you constantly asking yourself what to do next, where to place your shot to be safe, where to go to leave yourself in the best position . . . These and other fine points of strategy are the essence of the middle-distance game.

I have reserved until last one course where the par-fours may be among some of the greatest mysteries in golf. The course, as you may have guessed, is St Andrews.

We have already looked at two great finishing holes, so let us consider the 18th at St Andrews. On the face of it, if your life was at stake and you had to get a par-four to save it, this hole would be a favourite candidate. It looks the easiest thing in the world, and yet, and yet . . . We saw what happened to Doug Sanders in 1970. He had the Open Championship in his pocket. In all but name he had won it. At the 17th he got down in two from the Road Hole bunker when all the odds were against him, and then all he needed was a four at the 18th to win. He hit a beautiful drive, put his second on the back of the green – and three-putted. That forced him into a play-off, with Nicklaus, which he lost.

If you analyze the hole, there seems to be nothing to it. No bunkers. Just a big hollow in front of the left side of the green – named, for all that, the Valley of Sin. Even so, where's the problem? Can't see it. Doddle. Got to be . . .

The 18th at St. Andrews

You hit your drive and walk up, and then you begin to feel the impact of several things. Your own tiredness, perhaps, especially if the wind has been blowing. The history of the place starts to get to you — straight in front are the famous clubhouse, the clock, the old grey town. Plus, perhaps, a few spectators, just at a time when you would rather not have to perform in public. And then there's the enormous green, measuring something like 120 yards across. It looks a doddle, but why are you tense? No, a four to finish at St Andrews is a hole well played.

St Andrews has firmly stood the test of more than two hundred years. Very little has been changed in that time. You can even play the Old Course from back to front, starting at the 1st tee and going to the 17th green, then on to the 18th tee and the 16th green, and so on, which is remarkable enough. The breadth of the whole place, with its double greens, is something that always impresses the pro golfer coming to the course for the first time, and perhaps inclines him to think that 'there's nothing here'. Then he starts to play, and the extraordinary cunning of the layout soon becomes clear.

Perhaps the greatest of St Andrews's secrets is locked away in those vast greens, which are quite unlike greens anywhere else. With all the variations of pin placement available, you can be on the green and yet still 40 yards from the hole. It is hardly surprising, given also the great variations in pace and contour, that people take three putts from time to time. On the other hand, three-putting is something you really should try very hard to avoid on a course which has fourteen par-fours. That's the trap, you see. That's where they get you.

Rounds Played

ROUND NO	COURSE											SSS		DATE			

PLAYING WITH

PLAYING AGAINST

COMPETITION						WEATHER											

TEES PLAYED OFF						TIME											

HOLE NO	1	2	3	4	5	6	7	8	9	10	11	12	13	14	15	16	17	18
PAR																		
SELF																		
OPPONENT																		
RESULT																		
TOTAL	OUT		IN			GROSS			HANDICAP				NETT				

MATCH/COMPETITION RESULT

COMMENTS

ROUND NO	COURSE											SSS		DATE			

PLAYING WITH

PLAYING AGAINST

COMPETITION						WEATHER											

TEES PLAYED OFF						TIME											

HOLE NO	1	2	3	4	5	6	7	8	9	10	11	12	13	14	15	16	17	18
PAR																		
SELF																		
OPPONENT																		
RESULT																		
TOTAL	OUT		IN			GROSS			HANDICAP				NETT				

MATCH/COMPETITION RESULT

COMMENTS

Jack Hoag said: 'In golf, more than in any other game, a player is forced to recognize that "thoughts are acts". Success or failure entirely depends on your own state of mind.'

ROUND NO	COURSE										SSS					DATE		
PLAYING WITH																		
PLAYING AGAINST																		
COMPETITION							WEATHER											
TEES PLAYED OFF							TIME											

HOLE NO	1	2	3	4	5	6	7	8	9	10	11	12	13	14	15	16	17	18
PAR																		
SELF																		
OPPONENT																		
RESULT																		

TOTAL	OUT		IN			GROSS			HANDICAP				NETT	

MATCH/COMPETITION RESULT

COMMENTS

ROUND NO	COURSE										SSS					DATE		
PLAYING WITH																		
PLAYING AGAINST																		
COMPETITION							WEATHER											
TEES PLAYED OFF							TIME											

HOLE NO	1	2	3	4	5	6	7	8	9	10	11	12	13	14	15	16	17	18
PAR																		
SELF																		
OPPONENT																		
RESULT																		

TOTAL	OUT		IN			GROSS			HANDICAP				NETT	

MATCH/COMPETITION RESULT

COMMENTS

Alex Herd: 'Cut out the tee shot from golf and there would not be enough left to keep the game going. You might just as well take the whisky out of the soda.'

ROUND NO	COURSE									SSS					DATE		

PLAYING WITH

PLAYING AGAINST

COMPETITION						WEATHER											

TEES PLAYED OFF						TIME											

HOLE NO	1	2	3	4	5	6	7	8	9	10	11	12	13	14	15	16	17	18
PAR																		
SELF																		
OPPONENT																		
RESULT																		

TOTAL	OUT		IN			GROSS				HANDICAP					NETT		

MATCH/COMPETITION RESULT

COMMENTS

ROUND NO	COURSE									SSS					DATE		

PLAYING WITH

PLAYING AGAINST

COMPETITION						WEATHER											

TEES PLAYED OFF						TIME											

HOLE NO	1	2	3	4	5	6	7	8	9	10	11	12	13	14	15	16	17	18
PAR																		
SELF																		
OPPONENT																		
RESULT																		

TOTAL	OUT		IN			GROSS				HANDICAP					NETT		

MATCH/COMPETITION RESULT

COMMENTS

George Ganz said: 'Always concentrate on seeing your putter's face hit the ball and wait to hear the rattle in the tin.'

ROUND NO	COURSE												SSS			DATE		
PLAYING WITH																		
PLAYING AGAINST																		
COMPETITION								WEATHER										
TEES PLAYED OFF								TIME										
HOLE NO	1	2	3	4	5	6	7	8	9	10	11	12	13	14	15	16	17	18
PAR																		
SELF																		
OPPONENT																		
RESULT																		
TOTAL	OUT			IN			GROSS			HANDICAP				NETT				
MATCH/COMPETITION RESULT																		
COMMENTS																		

ROUND NO	COURSE												SSS			DATE		
PLAYING WITH																		
PLAYING AGAINST																		
COMPETITION								WEATHER										
TEES PLAYED OFF								TIME										
HOLE NO	1	2	3	4	5	6	7	8	9	10	11	12	13	14	15	16	17	18
PAR																		
SELF																		
OPPONENT																		
RESULT																		
TOTAL	OUT			IN			GROSS			HANDICAP				NETT				
MATCH/COMPETITION RESULT																		
COMMENTS																		

Walter Hagen: 'The timing of the stroke is done as much with the feet as with the hands or the body.'

ROUND NO	COURSE													SSS		DATE	
PLAYING WITH																	
PLAYING AGAINST																	
COMPETITION						WEATHER											
TEES PLAYED OFF						TIME											

HOLE NO	1	2	3	4	5	6	7	8	9	10	11	12	13	14	15	16	17	18
PAR																		
SELF																		
OPPONENT																		
RESULT																		

TOTAL	OUT		IN			GROSS			HANDICAP				NETT		

MATCH/COMPETITION RESULT

COMMENTS

ROUND NO	COURSE													SSS		DATE	
PLAYING WITH																	
PLAYING AGAINST																	
COMPETITION						WEATHER											
TEES PLAYED OFF						TIME											

HOLE NO	1	2	3	4	5	6	7	8	9	10	11	12	13	14	15	16	17	18
PAR																		
SELF																		
OPPONENT																		
RESULT																		

TOTAL	OUT		IN			GROSS			HANDICAP				NETT		

MATCH/COMPETITION RESULT

COMMENTS

Other Courses Played

Find out as much as you can about the courses you visit. Store any useful information away and try and learn a little bit about the club's history. It is not a bad idea to keep a camera in the car so that you can record the clubhouse, or take a picture of their famous professional, or club dog which has found 94,000 balls and bought 74 wheelchairs for the old folks in the home on the hill.

COURSE _____ (SEE ROUND NO ___)

ADDRESS _____

SECRETARY _____ TELEPHONE _____

PROFESSIONAL _____ TELEPHONE _____

STARTING TIMES & BOOKING PROCEDURE _____

GREEN FEES _____ CADDY FEES _____

LOCATION/ HOW TO GET THERE _____

CLUB FACILITIES _____

LOCAL ACCOMMODATION/RESTAURANTS _____

___ CLUB HISTORY ___

MAJOR COMPETITIONS HELD ON THE COURSE

_____

FAMOUS MEMBERS & GREAT CHARACTERS

_____

COMMENTS _____

FAVOURITE HOLES _____

___ COURSE RECORD ___

AMATEUR	SCORE	PROFESSIONAL	SCORE

COURSE _____ (SEE ROUND NO _____)

ADDRESS _____

SECRETARY _____ TELEPHONE _____

PROFESSIONAL _____ TELEPHONE _____

STARTING TIMES & BOOKING PROCEDURE _____

GREEN FEES _____ CADDY FEES _____

LOCATION/HOW TO GET THERE _____

CLUB FACILITIES _____

LOCAL ACCOMMODATION/RESTAURANTS _____

—————————— CLUB HISTORY ——————————
MAJOR COMPETITIONS HELD ON THE COURSE

—————— FAMOUS MEMBERS & GREAT CHARACTERS ——————

COMMENTS _____

FAVOURITE HOLES _____

—————————— COURSE RECORD ——————————

AMATEUR	SCORE	PROFESSIONAL	SCORE

COURSE _____ (SEE ROUND NO __)

ADDRESS _____

_____

SECRETARY _____ TELEPHONE _____

PROFESSIONAL _____ TELEPHONE _____

STARTING TIMES & BOOKING PROCEDURE _____

_____

GREEN FEES _____ CADDY FEES _____

LOCATION / HOW TO GET THERE _____

CLUB FACILITIES _____

LOCAL ACCOMMODATION/RESTAURANTS _____

_____

——————————— CLUB HISTORY ———————————
MAJOR COMPETITIONS HELD ON THE COURSE

_____

_____

FAMOUS MEMBERS & GREAT CHARACTERS

_____

_____

COMMENTS _____

_____

FAVOURITE HOLES _____

——————————— COURSE RECORD ———————————

AMATEUR	SCORE	PROFESSIONAL	SCORE

COURSE _____ (SEE ROUND NO   )

ADDRESS _____

SECRETARY _____   TELEPHONE _____

PROFESSIONAL _____   TELEPHONE _____

STARTING TIMES & BOOKING PROCEDURE _____

_____

GREEN FEES _____   CADDY FEES _____

LOCATION / HOW TO GET THERE _____

CLUB FACILITIES _____

LOCAL ACCOMMODATION/RESTAURANTS _____

_____

_____

———————————————— CLUB HISTORY ————————————————
MAJOR COMPETITIONS HELD ON THE COURSE _____

_____

_____

FAMOUS MEMBERS & GREAT CHARACTERS _____

_____

_____

_____

COMMENTS _____

_____

FAVOURITE HOLES _____

———————————————— COURSE RECORD ————————————————

AMATEUR	SCORE	PROFESSIONAL	SCORE

COURSE _____ (SEE ROUND NO ____)

ADDRESS _____

_____

SECRETARY _____ TELEPHONE _____

PROFESSIONAL _____ TELEPHONE _____

STARTING TIMES & BOOKING PROCEDURE _____

_____

GREEN FEES _____ CADDY FEES _____

LOCATION / HOW TO GET THERE _____

CLUB FACILITIES _____

LOCAL ACCOMMODATION/RESTAURANTS _____

_____

_____

———————————— CLUB HISTORY ————————————

MAJOR COMPETITIONS HELD ON THE COURSE

_____

_____

FAMOUS MEMBERS & GREAT CHARACTERS

_____

_____

_____

COMMENTS _____

_____

FAVOURITE HOLES _____

———————————— COURSE RECORD ————————————

AMATEUR	SCORE	PROFESSIONAL	SCORE

COURSE   (SEE ROUND NO   )

ADDRESS

SECRETARY   TELEPHONE

PROFESSIONAL   TELEPHONE

STARTING TIMES & BOOKING PROCEDURE

GREEN FEES   CADDY FEES

LOCATION / HOW TO GET THERE

CLUB FACILITIES

LOCAL ACCOMMODATION/RESTAURANTS

───── CLUB HISTORY ─────
MAJOR COMPETITIONS HELD ON THE COURSE

FAMOUS MEMBERS & GREAT CHARACTERS

COMMENTS

FAVOURITE HOLES

───── COURSE RECORD ─────

AMATEUR	SCORE	PROFESSIONAL	SCORE

COURSE _____ (SEE ROUND NO _____)

ADDRESS _____

SECRETARY _____ TELEPHONE _____

PROFESSIONAL _____ TELEPHONE _____

STARTING TIMES & BOOKING PROCEDURE _____

GREEN FEES _____ CADDY FEES _____

LOCATION / HOW TO GET THERE _____

CLUB FACILITIES _____

LOCAL ACCOMMODATION/RESTAURANTS _____

──────────────── CLUB HISTORY ────────────────
MAJOR COMPETITIONS HELD ON THE COURSE

FAMOUS MEMBERS & GREAT CHARACTERS

COMMENTS _____

FAVOURITE HOLES _____

──────────────── COURSE RECORD ────────────────

AMATEUR	SCORE	PROFESSIONAL	SCORE

COURSE _____ (SEE ROUND NO   )

ADDRESS _____

SECRETARY _____ TELEPHONE _____

PROFESSIONAL _____ TELEPHONE _____

STARTING TIMES & BOOKING PROCEDURE _____

GREEN FEES _____ CADDY FEES _____

LOCATION / HOW TO GET THERE _____

CLUB FACILITIES _____

LOCAL ACCOMMODATION/RESTAURANTS _____

——————————— CLUB HISTORY ———————————
MAJOR COMPETITIONS HELD ON THE COURSE

FAMOUS MEMBERS & GREAT CHARACTERS

COMMENTS _____

FAVOURITE HOLES _____

——————————— COURSE RECORD ———————————

AMATEUR	SCORE	PROFESSIONAL	SCORE

COURSE _____ (SEE ROUND NO   )

ADDRESS _____

_____

SECRETARY _____ TELEPHONE _____

PROFESSIONAL _____ TELEPHONE _____

STARTING TIMES & BOOKING PROCEDURE _____

_____

GREEN FEES _____ CADDY FEES _____

LOCATION / HOW TO GET THERE _____

CLUB FACILITIES _____

LOCAL ACCOMMODATION/RESTAURANTS _____

_____

_____

—————————— CLUB HISTORY ——————————
MAJOR COMPETITIONS HELD ON THE COURSE _____

_____

_____

FAMOUS MEMBERS & GREAT CHARACTERS _____

_____

_____

COMMENTS _____

_____

FAVOURITE HOLES _____

—————————— COURSE RECORD ——————————

AMATEUR	SCORE	PROFESSIONAL	SCORE

COURSE _____ (SEE ROUND NO   )

ADDRESS _____

_____

SECRETARY _____ TELEPHONE _____

PROFESSIONAL _____ TELEPHONE _____

STARTING TIMES & BOOKING PROCEDURE _____

_____

GREEN FEES _____ CADDY FEES _____

LOCATION/HOW TO GET THERE _____

CLUB FACILITIES _____

LOCAL ACCOMMODATION/RESTAURANTS _____

_____

_____

———————— CLUB HISTORY ————————
MAJOR COMPETITIONS HELD ON THE COURSE

_____

_____

FAMOUS MEMBERS & GREAT CHARACTERS

_____

_____

_____

COMMENTS _____

_____

FAVOURITE HOLES _____

———————— COURSE RECORD ————————

AMATEUR	SCORE	PROFESSIONAL	SCORE

Support Your Local Pro

What you need is a relationship. From the moment you decide to take up the game, try to involve your local club professional. If you are an absolute beginner, tell him. There is no point in blaring on about the couple of rounds you played just after you left school twenty years ago, but which you have never forgotten. Simply go along with a smile on your face and say: 'Hello, I'm Joe Smith and I'm thinking of taking up the game of golf. Can you help me?'

The golf professional has been with us now for over a hundred years and I feel – not merely because I used to be one myself – that he is worth preserving. All club golfers need a little bit of coaching every now and then. They are amateurs, and only the very lucky ones are free to play whenever they want. Naturally the average member gets out of practice and develops bad habits – and these, amongst his other duties, are what the club pro is there to cure.

If, as an established member or a beginner, you don't find the pro particularly keen or cooperative, go elsewhere. There used to be a strong general feeling that, as with doctors, it wasn't done to change your golf pro. If old Mackenzie was your doctor, it was irrelevant that he was a pain in the neck and rotten at his job; he was your doctor and you stuck with him, in sickness and in health. The modern view seems to be that all professional services should give proper value, golf included, and it is not a sin to shop around, collecting advice from many different sources – and taking your golf lessons from the man in whom you have the most confidence. After all, if this is to be your game for a lifetime, it is worth taking the trouble from the outset.

Most professionals understand this, and are only too pleased to respond to the right approach. If you support professional golfers, they will support you, and this is especially valuable when you are starting out and need advice on everything under the sun – which clubs suit your height, weight and general build, which golf balls are best, which shoes, bags, waterproofs, etc, etc. If the relationship is right, the pro can help you enormously from the very beginning – with preliminary tuition, for instance, while you are deciding whether you actually want to take up the game as a serious hobby and invest all that money in equipment. If, on the other hand, you turn up at the club fully equipped and start telling the pro how clever you were buying them at a discount, you may find he suddenly has other things to do when you are around.

When that happens, you really have only yourself to blame, and there is little point in storming off to the professional at the next club down the road if you are merely going to repeat the performance with him.

Another side of the pro's job is to go out and play with the members. The days may be gone when the average member could regularly afford a round with the pro by himself, but that does not mean that the poor old pro has to be put out to grass. Why not club together with two other members and share the expense? Maybe the pro does not have time to complete a four-ball during which he has to rush hither and thither offering advice to the other three; if so, cut it to nine holes. It only takes half the time, but in the course of playing nine holes you are bound to demonstrate nearly all your strengths and weaknesses, and so there will still be an awful lot for the pro to teach you.

The pro shop, and its future, is a little more problematic. It is like the village store, which you either support or neglect in favour of the wonderful cut-price bargains at your nearest hypermarket. The nature of the pro shop, because of 'market forces' (that wondrous phrase beloved by economists) has changed dramatically in the last few years. Fifteen or twenty thousand pounds does not buy an awful lot of stock these days, and so the club pro has had to become much more specialized. He can run to one complete range of golf shoes, probably, but not to eight different makes plus a few pairs of these super-waterproof shoes and those super-de-luxe ones. His stock of clubs, balls, hats and so on will be similarly scaled down. If he is wise, he will stick mainly to the nuts and bolts of golfing equipment, and not be too bothered about the 'fashion' side of things.

The choice between him and the discount stores can, admittedly, be difficult. Into the scales on the pro's side you should nevertheless allow something for the benefits of personal service. He, at least, knows you and your habits – or is beginning to – and is in the best position to fit you out with equipment that you can use, and use profitably. In that sense you should be wary of cut-price offers, or of buying cheap from a friend. If you were looking for a car, and James Hunt came along and said he was selling off his old racer for £750, would you want it? Frankly, you wouldn't know how to start it, and if you did, and managed to get it into gear, you would still end up spinning it in the middle of the road at 100 mph, which is really rather a waste of time. It may have seemed an attractive proposition when you first heard of it, but it isn't because it won't do the job that you want it to.

This is an area where it is more than useful to see what the tournament professionals do. In today's world, where so much equipment is on offer, a lot of it well advertised, and attractive too – perhaps because it is a little different or experimental – the great players nevertheless remain very conventional. Very few of the top players go in for clubs with funny necks, fancy colours and bits of decoration. They have their problems, of course, and each year you notice a fresh crop of weird and wonderful solutions, viz. Bernhard Langer's 'wrong-handed' grip for short puts which he has been using side by side with a conventional grip for longer putts. That, however, is more a question of mental approach. Langer is not saying there is anything wrong with his putter, which is perfectly conventional. He has identified the problem as being one that resides in his head, and has not resorted to some space-age device with holes in it and a radar aerial in the hope that this will make the putts go in.

Your local pro well understands these funny quirks and temptations. He spends his working life surrounded by them. And that is why you need him.

Golfing Equipment

Here you must decide whether you are an experimenter, and therefore the golf professional's friend, or do you still swear by that thirty- or forty-year-old set of clubs

--- WOODS ---

--- IRONS ---

--- PUTTERS ---

--- GOLF BALLS ---

--- GOLF BAGS AND TROLLEYS ---

passed down to you via Dad from Grandad? In either case you can use these pages to catalogue your current equipment, adding your comments on how effective or otherwise you have found each item to be. Do you in fact remember the first set of clubs you ever had, the putter you thought was going to fulfil all your hopes, and now has somehow vanished or collects dust under the stairs? Put them all down here.

───── OTHER ITEMS OF EQUIPMENT THAT YOU KEEP IN YOUR GOLF BAG ─────

───── SHOES ─────

───── HATS/CAPS ─────

───── WATERPROOFS ─────

───── OTHER CLOTHING YOU FIND PARTICULARLY USEFUL, WARM, LUCKY, ETC ─────

Start a Collection

The field of golf collectables is as wide as you care to make it. Just think of all the stuff that is on view in the tented village at a big tournament. They, if you like, are the stockrooms of tomorrow's antique shops. And don't forget all the printed bits and pieces which you automatically collect, starting with car park stickers and entrance tickets and ending I don't know where – hospitality vouchers, button badges, tiepins, pennants, the latest line in giveaways from a company day out . . .

Sarah Baddiel, an avid collector, of whom more below, has T-shirts from the 1983 US Open. She also has a Suntory beer can, specially brewed for one of the tournaments sponsored by the company and featuring little silver golfers who circle the 350 ml can, each at a different stage of a golf stroke. (Incidentally, if you are interested in collecting that kind of item, Sarah tells me that cans and bottles are more valuable if you leave the liquor inside!)

Some people might find that sort of object a bit ephemeral. One line of collecting that is consistently popular with golf enthusiasts is books. Over the page we have left space for you to make a list of your present and future acquisitions. First of all, though, let's see what categories of golfing book might interest a beginner.

If you like fine writing, you will almost certainly be on the lookout for anything by Bernard Darwin, golf correspondent of *The Times* and *Country Life* for many years and whose first book, *The Golf Courses of Great Britain*, appeared in 1925 and was followed by many a minor classic, including *The Game's Afoot* (1926), *Out of the Rough* (1932) and *Green Memories* (1933). P.G. Wodehouse wrote some funny pieces about golf, and most enthusiasts would also want something in their collection by those great correspondents of modern times, Pat Ward-Thomas, Henry Longhurst and Herbert Warren Wind.

Nearly all the big names have written autobiographies, and that is a good area to delve into. From times past, seek out books by Bobby Jones, Walter Hagen and Ben Hogan, whose *Power Golf* (1949) is much quoted to this day. Among the great modern players, you may as well choose your favourites and see if you can find their version of how they made it to the top. It is always useful to have one or two tuitional books in the house, and you could not do much better than read those by Henry Cotton and John Jacobs.

Golf equipment is another popular line with collectors. At the top end of the market you can be operating in expensive company: an old club, for instance, recently fetched £2,000 at St Andrews. On the other hand, you don't have to spend the earth to build yourself an attractive collection. About ten years ago Bob Jamieson, a friend of mine and the professional at Turnberry, started a collection of golf balls for his son. Every time a golf ball was on the verge of going extinct, he bought a dozen and stored them away, brand new, wrapped in paper in their original box. Since he began, there have been at least forty such changes, and in years to come that collection will be of enormous interest – and great value.

Prints and posters are good to collect, frame and hang on the wall at home. These are getting harder to find, however, and it might be more rewarding to switch your researches into early golf photographs, or cigarette cards. Have a look at your local club's treasures and see if these suggest a line of approach. Over the years, few crafts have not at some time used a golf theme. Thus, if you look long enough, you will find silver, pottery and china with a golfing pattern or motif, golf games and tin toys. Sarah Baddiel has a golf ball which you wind up and it waddles along – perfect for the golfer who has everything else, I would have thought! Anyway, the field is broad and there is always room for another collector. Below are some names and addresses which you may find useful.

Publications about collecting

Don Kennington and Sarah Baddiel, *The Sourcebook of Golf*, available from Sarah Baddiel (see below).

J.S.F. Murdoch (ed.) *The Golf Collectors Society Bulletin*, available by subscription from the editor, 638 Wagner Road, Lafayette Hill, Pa 19444, USA.

Golf books

Richard Donovan, 305 Massachusetts Avenue, Endicott, New York 13760, USA.

Golf books and other collectables

Sarah Baddiel, Golfiana, The Book Gallery, Grays Antique Market, Davies Mews, Brook Street, London W1; tel 01-408 1239 or 01-452 7243.

THE GOLFER'S LOGBOOK

Golf Library

Collecting books on golf has become quite a popular hobby, and although it has grown expensive over the years it is still possible for you to establish a reasonable collection at a

TITLE & AUTHOR	COMMENTS

fairly modest price. Many of you no doubt already own books which have been helpful to you or given you enjoyment. I suggest you list these below and then add others as you go along.

TITLE & AUTHOR	COMMENTS

Autographs

If you enjoy collecting autographs, reserve these two pages for some of the great and interesting names in the game of golf. I always think it better – and you will get a far kinder response from whoever you approach – if you can produce a proper book for them to

write in, and a pen to do it with. Try, if you can, to avoid bringing with you the kind of companion who interrupts the magic of these moments by hissing: 'Who is it? Who is it?'

Home Course Eclectic

Whether or not your club runs an eclectic competition, why not keep track of your best score on each hole and see whether you can beat par, or indeed by how much. Now, if only you could string all those figures together in just one round! One man with a most curious record was Joe Close, an early mentor of mine at Ferndown. Among his many achievements Joe holed every short hole on that course in one, and every other hole in two – including the then 8th hole at 510 yards!

DATE											ECLECTIC SCORE	PAR
1												
2												
3												
4												
5												
6												
7												
8												
9												
OUT												
10												
11												
12												
13												
14												
15												
16												
17												
18												
IN												
OUT												
TOTAL												

Handicap Revisions

The current handicapping system, while it may seem overly complicated at times, does have the advantage of requiring regular revision. So it makes sense to keep your own record of any round that entails a revision to your *exact* handicap – from which, of course, your *playing* handicap is taken. By doing so, you will also have a better 'feel' at all times of how you are playing in relation to your handicap.

CURRENT HANDICAP			LOWEST EVER HANDICAP			CLUB		YEAR
DATE	SCORE	REVISED	DATE	SCORE	REVISED	DATE	SCORE	REVISED

Competition Record

Every golfer should try to sharpen his or her competitive edge. Enter as many competitions as you can, and watch your concentration and your golfing technique

ROUND No	DATE	COMPETITION	SCORING SYSTEM	SCORE	PRIZE, POSITION, COMMENTS

improve. There is nothing like competition to hone the game. How well I remember my putting escapades at Ferndown – putting for sixpence at a time when sixpence was *real* money!

ROUND No	DATE	COMPETITION	SCORING SYSTEM	SCORE	PRIZE, POSITION, COMMENTS

Medal Rounds

Don't forget to play regularly in medal rounds as this is probably the best way to keep an accurate handicap. But don't set out to be a bandit and don't fool yourself by hanging on to a handicap that you really can't play to. Also remember that if you are a bandit at the higher end of the scale – saying you're eighteen when you really play to twelve – it will cost you many friends, and in this day and age you will be soon found out!

ROUND NO	DATE	COMPETITION	GROSS	H/CAP	NETT	PRIZE, POSITION, COMMENTS

Golf Directory

And finally, if you have a problem or need extra guidance, why keep it to yourself? Use this selection of helping hands – some of golf's many august bodies and commercial specialists – to point you in the right direction.

Governing Bodies

Amateur

Royal and Ancient Golf Club of St Andrews, St Andrews, Fife; *0334 72112/3.*

English Golf Union, Secretary, 12a Denmark Street, Wokingham, Berkshire RG11 2BE; *0734 781952.*

Scottish Golf Union, Secretary, Bank of Scotland Building, 54 Shandwick Place, Edinburgh EH2 4RT; *031-266 6711.*

Welsh Golfing Union, Secretary, 2 Isfryn, Burry Point, Dyfed; *055-46 2595.*

Irish Golf Union, Secretary, Glencar House, 81 Eglington Road, Donnybrook, Dublin 4; *694111.*

English Ladies' Golf Association, Secretary, PO Box 14, 52 Boroughgate, Otley, West Yorkshire LS21 1QW; *0943 464010.*

Scottish Ladies' Golfing Association, Secretary, 1 Trinity Place, St Andrews, Fife; *0334 76849.*

Welsh Ladies' Golf Union, Hon. Secretary, Ysgoldy Gynt, Llanhennock, Newport, Gwent NP6 1LT; *0633 420642.*

Irish Ladies' Golf Union, Secretary, 44 Maretimo Gardens, E. Blackrock, Co. Dublin; *882542.*

English Schools' Golf Association, Hon. Secretary, Whickham Comprehensive School, Burnt House Lane, Whickham, Newcastle-upon-Tyne.

Scottish Schools' Golf Association, Hon. Secretary, Leith Academy Annexe, Albion Road, Edinburgh; *031-661 8277.*

Professional

The Professional Golfers' Association, Apollo House, The Belfry, Sutton Coldfield, West Midlands B76 9PT; *0675 70333.*

PGA European Tour, The Wentworth Club, Wentworth Drive, Virginia Water, Surrey GU25 4LS; *09904 2921.*

Women's Professional Golf Association, Apollo House, The Belfry, Sutton Coldfield, West Midlands B76 9PT; *0675 70333.*

Associations and Societies

General

Golf Foundation, 78 Third Avenue, Bush Hill Park, Enfield, Middlesex EN1 1BX; *01-363 1245*.

National Golf Clubs' Advisory Association, Secretary, Victoria Mill, Buxton Road, Bakewell, Derbyshire DE14 1DA; *062981 3844*.

Golf Clubs' Association, 94–96 Wigmore Street, London, W1; *01-935 0665*.

European Golf Association, Hon. Secretary, 69 Avenue Victor Hugo, 75783 Paris 16, France; *010-33-1-500 8261*.

Specialist

The British Association of Golf Course Architects, Hon. Secretary' Marlow Place, Station Road, Marlow, Buckinghamshire SL7 1NB; *062-84 72555*.

British Golf Greenkeepers' Association, Hon. Secretary, 7 Tentergate Close, Knaresborough, North Yorkshire HG5 9BJ; *0423 863851*.

Scottish and International Greenkeepers' Association, Secretary, 137 Saughtonhall Drive, Edinburgh EH12 5TS; *031-337 3689*.

International Greenkeepers' Association, Secretary, Via Golf, CH 6987 Caslano, Switzerland.

Golf Club Stewards' Association, Hon. Secretary, 50 The Park, St. Albans, Hertfordshire; *0727 57334*.

The Association of Golf Club Secretaries, Secretary, Victoria Mill, Buxton Road, Bakewell, Derbyshire DE14 1DA; *062981 4314*.

Playing

Artisan Golfers' Association, Hon. Secretary, 51 Rose Hill, Park West, Sutton, Surrey; *01-644 7037*.

The Golfers' Club, International House, Windmill Road, Sunbury-on-Thames, Middlesex TW16 7HR.

Golf Society of Great Britain, Gleneagles, Maddox Park, Little Bookham, Surrey KT23 3BW; *0372 54260*.

British Left-Handed Golfers' Society, Hon. Secretary, 5 Andrew Lane, High Lane, Stockport, Cheshire SK6 8HT; *06632 5572*.

One-Armed Golfers' Society, Hon. Secretary, 11 Caldwell Lane, Felling, Gateshead 10, Tyne and Wear; *0632 694742.*
Hole in One Golf Society, Secretary, 1 Vigilant Way, Gravesend, Kent; *0474 534298.*
Senior Golfers' Society, Secretary, Holly Bank, Linchmere, Haslemere, Surrey; *0428 723006.*

Driving Ranges

Ascot Lavender Park Golf Centre, Swinley Road, Ascot, Berkshire; *0344 4074.*
Belfast Knockbracken Golf Centre, Ballymaconaghy Road, Belfast; *0232 643554.*
Blackpool Phoenix Sporting and Leisure Centre, Fleetwood Road, Norbeck, Blackpool, Lancashire; *0235 4846.*
Bolton Kearsley Golf Range, Moss Lane, Kearsley, nr Bolton, Greater Manchester; *0204 75726.*
Chatham Chatham Golf Centre, Street-End Road, Chatham, Kent; *0634 48925.*
Chingford Chingford Golf Range, Waltham Way, Chingford, London E4.
Cobham Fairmile Hotel, Portsmouth Road, Cobham, Surrey; *09326 4419.*
Colchester Ardleigh Golf Range, Crown Inn, Ipswich Road, Ardleigh, Colchester, Essex; *0206 230211.*
Colnbrook Gallymead Golf Driving Range, Old Bath Road, Colnbrook, Buckinghamshire.
Coventry Coventry Golf Drive Centre, Sandpits Lane, Keresley, Coventry, West Midlands; *020-333 3405.*
Coventry Forest of Arden Driving Range, Maxstoke Lane, Meriden, Coventry; *0676 22118.*
Croydon Long Lane, Addiscombe, Surrey; *01-656 1690.*
Dublin John Jacobs Golf School, Foxrock; *Dublin 895341.*
Dublin Leopardstown Golf Centre, Foxrock; *Dublin 895341.*
Ealing Rowdell Road, Northolt, Middlesex; *01-845 4967.*
Edinburgh Port Royal Golf Range, Ingliston; *031-335 4377.*
Esher Sandown Golf Centre, Sandown Park, Moor Lane, Esher, Surrey; *0372 65921.*

Finchley High Road, Finchley, London N12; *01-445 0411.*
Gloucester Gloucester Country Club, Matson Lane, Gloucester; *0452 25653.*
Hamilton Strathclyde Park Golf Range, Hamilton, Strathclyde.
Horam Eastfields Golf Complex, Chiddingly Road, Horam, nr Heathfield, East Sussex; *04353 3355.*
Ipswich Ipswich Golf Range, Suffolk Show Ground, Bucklesham Road, Ipswich, Suffolk; *0473 76821.*
Jersey Western Golf Range, St Ouen Bay, Jersey.
Kingston-upon-Hull National Avenue, Kingston-upon-Hull, North Humberside; *0482 492720.*
Leatherhead Riverside Driving Range, River Lane, Fetcham, Leatherhead, Surrey; *0372 5713.*
Leicester Arnold Palmer Golf Range, Melton Road, Leicester; *0533 64400.*
London Abercorn Golf School, 27a Abercorn Place, London NW8.
Newcastle Gosforth Park Golf Centre, High Gosforth Park, Newcastle-upon-Tyne.
Newtownabbey Ballyearl Leisure Centre, 585 Doagh Road, Newtownabbey, Co. Antrim; *02313 7580.*
Newtownards Bradshaw's Brae Golf Centre Ltd, 115 Belfast Road, Killarn, Newtownards, Co. Down; *0247 813484.*
Northampton Delapre Golf Complex, Eagle Drive, Nene Valley Way, Northampton.
Norwich Norwich Golf Centre, Long Lane, Bawburgh, Norwich, Norfolk.
Nottingham Carlton Forum Golf Range, Foxhill Road, Carlton, Nottingham; *0602 871434.*
Old Woking Hoebridge Golf Centre, Old Woking, Surrey; *04862 22611/2.*
Orpington Ruxley Golf Centre, Sandy Lane, St Pauls Cray, Orpington, Kent; *0689 71490.*
Pease Pottage Fairway Golf Driving Range, Horsham Road, Pease Pottage, West Sussex; *0293 33000.*
Portsmouth Portsmouth Golf Centre, Eastern Road, Portsmouth, Hampshire; *0705 664549.*
Reading Sindlesham Driving Range, Mole Road, Winnersh, Reading, Berkshire; *0734 782139.*

Renfrew Normandy Golf Range, Renfrew, Strathclyde; *041-886 7477*.
Richmond Richmond Athletic Sports Ground, Chertsey Road, Richmond, Surrey.
Ripon Lightwater Valley Leisure Centre, Ripon, North Yorkshire; *0765 85321*.
Saffron Walden Little Walden Road, Saffron Walden, Essex; *0799 23339*.
St Neots St Neots Leisure Centre, Eynesbury, Hardwicke Golf Course, St Neots, Cambridgeshire; *0480 215153*.
Swindon Broome Manor Driving Range, Broome Manor Golf Complex, Pipers Way, Swindon, Wiltshire; *0793 32403*.
Tilsworth Broad Range Golf and Leisure Centre, Dunstable Road, Tilsworth, Bedfordshire; *995 210271/2*.
Uddingston Clydeway Golf Range, Blantyre Farm Road, Uddingston, Lanarkshire; *041-641 8899*.
Wadhurst Dale Hill Driving Range, Ticehurst, Wadhurst, East Sussex; *0580 200112*.
Warwick Warwick Golf Centre, Racecourse, Warwick; *0926 44316*.
Washington George Washington Hotel, Stone Cellar Road, Washington, Tyne and Wear; *0632 472626*.
Watford Watford Driving Range, Sheepcot Lane, Garston, Watford, Hertfordshire; *09273 75560*.
Welwyn Garden City Welwyn Hatfield Sports Centre, Driving Range, Stanborough Road, Welwyn Garden City, Hertfordshire; *07073 31056*.
Wokingham Downshire Golf Club, Easthampstead Park, Wokingham, Berkshire; *0344 24066*.
Wolverhampton Three Hammers Golf Centre, Coven, nr Wolverhampton, West Midlands.

Hotels
with their own
Golf Course

England

Cambridge Cunard Cambridgeshire Hotel, Bar Hill, Cambridge; *0954 80555.*

Canterbury Broome Park Golf and Country Club, Barham, Canterbury, Kent CT4 6QX; *022782 771.*

Cromer The Links Country Park Hotel, West Runton, Cromer, Norfolk NR27 9QH; *026375 691.*

Dorking Gatton Manor Hotel, Ockley, Dorking, Surrey RH5 5PQ; *030679 555.*

Falmouth Budock Vean Hotel, Falmouth, Cornwall; *0326 288.*

Gloucester Gloucester Hotel and Country Club, Robinswood Hill, Gloucester; *0452 25653.*

Kingsbridge Thurlestone Hotel, Thurlestone, Kingsbridge, South Devon TQ7 3NN; *0548 560382.*

Liphook Old Thornes Golf and Country Club, Longmoor Road, Liphook, Hampshire; *0428 724555.*

Morley Breadsall Priory Hotel, Moor Road, Morley, Derbyshire; *0332 832235.*

Moretonhampstead The Manor House Hotel, Moretonhampstead, Devon; *06474 355.*

Norwich Barnham Broom Hotel, Norwich NR9 4DD; *060545 437.*

Padstow Trevose Golf and Country Club, Constantine Bay, Padstow, Cornwall; *0841 520202.*

St Austell The Carlyon Bay Hotel, St Austell, Cornwall; *072681 2304.*

Sanderstead Selsdon Park Hotel, Sanderstead, South Croydon, Surrey; *01-657 8811.*

Scarborough Raven Hall Hotel, Ravenscar, Scarborough, North Yorkshire.

Seaford The Dormy House, Seaford Golf Club, East Blatchington, Seaford, East Sussex BN25 2JD; *0323 892422.*

Shedfield Meon Valley Hotel, Sandy Lane, Shedfield, Southampton SO3 2HQ; *0329 833455.*

Shrewsbury Hawkestone Park Hotel, Weston-under-Redcastle, Shrewsbury SY4 5UY; *093924 611.*

Stratford-upon-Avon Welcombe Hotel, Warwick Road, Stratford-upon-Avon, Warwickshire CV37 0NR; *0789 295252.*

Telford Telford Hotel, Great Hay, Sutton Hill, Telford TF7 4DT; *0952 585642.*

Tewkesbury Tewkesbury Park Hotel, Lincoln Green Lane, Tewkesbury GL20 7DN; *0684 295405.*

Torpoint Whitsand Bay Hotel, Portwinkle, Torpoint, Cornwall PL11 3BU; *0503 30276.*

Ware Briggens House Hotel, Stanstead Abbotts, Ware, Hertfordshire SG12 8LD; *027979 2416.*

Wales
Chepstow St Pierre Hotel, St Pierre Park, Gwent NP6 6YA; *02912 5261.*

Scotland
Auchterarder Gleneagles Hotel, Auchterarder, Perthshire; *07646 3543.*

Kinross Green Hotel, Beeches Park, Kinross, Kinross-shire; *0577 63467.*

Turnberry Turnberry Hotel, Turnberry, Ayrshire; *06553 202.*

Ireland
Howth Deer Park Hotel, Howth, Co. Dublin; *322624.*

Travel Companies
which organize
<u>Golfing Holidays</u>

Bena Golf, Jordangate House, Jordangate, Macclesfield, Greater Manchester; *0625 617513.*
Blue Arrow Golf Holidays, Blue Arrow House, Camp Road, St Albans, Hertfordshire; *0727 69209.*
Caravela Tours, 38–44 Gillingham Street, London SW1; *01-630 5366.*
Eurogolf, 41 Watford Way, London NW4 3JH; *01-202 4744.*
Golfwings Holidays, Twickenham Travel, 84 Hampton Road, Twickenham, Middlesex TW2 5QS; *01-898 8351.*
Horizon Golf Holidays, Broadway, Edgbaston Five Ways, Birmingham B15 1BB; *021-632 6282.*
Insport Consultants, Bagshot House, High Street, Bagshot, Surrey GU19 5AF; *0276 73736.*
John Hill Golf Holidays, 223 Lower Mortlake Road, Richmond, Surrey; *01-948 4146.*
Longshot Golf Holidays, 135 Greenford Road, Sudbury Hill, Harrow, Middlesex HA1 3QN; *01-423 0400.*
Meridian Golf, 12–16 Dering Street, London W1R 9AB; *01-493 2777.*
Parasol Holidays, 24 Orchard Street, Crawley, Sussex RH11 7AF; *0293 514511.*
Sol Golf, Norwest Court, Guildhall Street, Preston, Lancashire PR1 3NU; *0772 555000.*
Sovereign Golf Holidays – British Airways; through all travel agents.
3D Golf Promotion, 62 Carcluie Crescent, Woodlea, Ayr KA7 4SZ; *0292 42206.*
Top Golf Holidays, 276 Preston Road, Harrow, Middlesex; *01-904 2202.*
Wings Golf, Wings House, High Road, Broxbourne, Hertfordshire EN10 7HX; *01-444 0007.*

Equipment Manufacturers

Clubs

Peter Broadbent, Persimmon House, Lysander Road, Bowerhill, Melksham, Wiltshire SN1 5SP; *0225 704056.*

Browning Sports Ltd, 37 Milton Trading Estate, Milton, nr Abingdon, Oxon; *0235 848122.*

Cobra Golf UK Ltd, PO Box 26, Knowle, Solihull, West Midlands B93 8EN; *05645 3357.*

Daiwa Golf (Scotland) Ltd, Tantallan Road, North Berwick, EH39 5NF; *0620 2219.*

Dunlop Sports Co. Ltd, Wakefield 41, West Yorkshire WF2 0XD; *0924 829393.*

Dyka, Metmac International Ltd, PO Box 128, London SW19 3DZ; *01-588 8721.*

Ben Hogan, E.J. Price Ltd, Porter Street, Dudley, West Midlands DY2 7RL; *0384 214247.*

John Letters & Co. (1918) Ltd, 1–3 Earl Haig Road, Hillington Industrial Estate, Glasgow G52 4JU; *041-882 9923.*

Lynx, Trendan Sports Ltd, Bell Lane, Uckfield, East Sussex TN22 1QL; *0825 61266.*

Macgregor Golf (UK) Ltd, Macgregor House, Ruddock Road, Caversham, Reading, Berkshire RG4 0BY.

Mizuno (UK) Ltd, Unit 3, Nimrod Way, Elgar Road, Reading, Berkshire RG2 0EB; *0734 752636.*

Toney Penna, Jupiter Sports Ltd, 209 Seaview Road, Wallasey, Merseyside L45 4DP; *051-639 8582.*

Ping, Karsten (UK) Ltd, Corringham Road, Gainsborough, Lincolnshire DN21 1XZ.

Ram Golf Corp., Trendan Sports Ltd, Bell Lane, Uckfield, East Sussex TN22 1QL; *0825 61266.*

Ryder Manufacturing Co. Ltd, 406 Hillington Road, Hillington Estate, Glasgow G52 4NG.

Ben Sayers, 1 Tantallon Road, North Berwick, East Lothian; *0620 2219.*

Slazengers Ltd, Challenge House, Mitcham Road, Croydon CR9 3AU; *01-684 3644.*

Sounder, Prosport Ltd, 9 Sedgeley Park Trading Estate, Prestwich,
Manchester M25 8WD; *061-798 8537.*
Spalding, Greenway Sports Ltd, Viking Way, Bar Hill Industrial Estate,
Cambridge CB3 8EL.
Stix, Kilbride Golf Manufacturing Co. Ltd, Unit 1, Turfholm Industrial
Estate, Lesmahagow, Lanark; *0555 893971/893218.*
Swilken of St Andrews, Stewart Works, Tom Stewart Lane, St Andrews,
Fife KY16 8XW; *0334 72266.*
Tiger Shark, Sigma Golf (UK) Ltd, Matson Lane, Gloucester GL4 9EA;
0452 411331.
Titleist, Acushnet Ltd, Orchard Road, Great Shelford, Cambridge
CB2 5AB; *0223 842751.*
Wilson Sporting Goods Co. Ltd, Ayr Road, Irvine, Ayrshire KA12 8HG;
0294 87244.
Yamaha, William Ling & Associates Ltd, Unit 4, Osiers Industrial Estate,
Enterprise Way, Osiers Road, London SW18 1NL; *01-871 0998/9.*

Gloves
Aristocrat, George Jefferies Gloves, Fairfield Road, Warminster,
Wiltshire; *0985 212716.*
Kasco, Kamatari (UK) Ltd, Unit 20, The Forbury Industrial Park,
Kenavon Drive, Reading, Berkshire RG1 3HS; *0734 508616.*

Grips
Charger Pro-Cushion, Avon Industrial Polymers Ltd, Melksham,
Wiltshire SN12 8AA; *0225 703101.*
Lamkin Leather and Rubber Co. Ltd, Dereham House, Tilford, Farnham,
Surrey GU10 2DD.

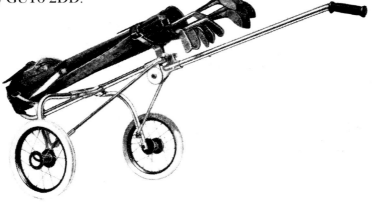

Bags

Kin Bag (UK), Appledore Road, Tenterden, Kent TN30 7BE; *05807 2047*.
Rola Sport Ltd, Brook House, South Street, Brentwood, Essex CM14 4BA; *0277 232896*.
Supadivida, E.J. Price Ltd, Porter Street, Dudley, West Midlands DY2 7RL; *0384 214247*.
Trolee Bag, Willersey, Broadway, Hereford and Worcester WR12 7PR; *0386 852013*.

Power Trolleys

Auto Caddie, Tee Caddie (Golf Equipment) Ltd, 36 Foregate Street, Astwood Bank, Redditch, Hereford and Worcester B96 6BW; *052789 3720*.
Kangaroo Motor Golf Caddies, Kangaroo Products Co., 284 Birmingham Factory Centre, Kings Norton, Birmingham B30 3HN; *021-451 1163*.
Powa Kaddy Products, Sittingbourne Industrial Park, Crown Quay Lane, Sittingbourne, Kent ME10 3JH; *0795 26040*.
'Sherpa' Electric Caddy, Woodhams Engineering, PO Box 36, Horley, Surrey RH6 7RG; *02934 4439*.
Cadd'x, 139a Sloane Street, London SW1X 9AY; *01-730 9958*.

Sportswear

Burberry's Ltd, 145 Regent Street, London W1R 8AS; *01-734 5929*.
Farah Manufacturing (UK) Ltd, Unit 3, Lowfield Heath Distribution Centre, Charlwood Road, Crawley, West Sussex RH11 0JS; *0293 579282*.
Glenmuir Sportswear, Delves Road, Lanark, Scotland ML11 9DX; *0555 2241*.
Golf Girl International Ltd, Ryon Hill House, Warwick Road, Stratford-upon-Avon, Warwickshire CV37 0NZ; *0789 298690*.
Lyle & Scott, Lynnwood Factory, Liddesdale Road, Hawick, Roxburghshire; *0450 73361*.
Marlborough Leisure Wear, Master's Yard, 180 South Street, Dorking, Surrey RH42 2ES; *0306 887387*.
Munsingwear, Trendan Sports Ltd, Bell Lane, Uckfield, East Sussex TN22 1QL; *0825 61266*.

Pickering, Phoenixville, USA.
Pringle, Dawson International Ltd, Hawick, Scotland TD9 7AL.
Wolsey, Abbey Meadows, Leicester LE4 5AD; *0533 26073.*

Waterproofs
Dober Sportswear, 25 Upton Lane, Forest Gate, London E7 9PA; *01-552 8912.*
Le Sport, Trendan Sports Ltd, Bell Lane, Uckfield, East Sussex
TN22 1QL; *0825 61266.*
Playdri Products Ltd, Stanton, Bury St Edmunds, Suffolk; *0359 51420.*
Proquip, RCR Associates, Zone Works, Uley Road, Dursley,
Gloucestershire GL11 4AP.
Peter Storm, 14 High Pavement, Nottingham; *0602 506911.*
Sunderland Sportswear Ltd, PO Box, Glasgow, Scotland.

Shoes
Footjoy, Wentworth Sports, 12 Station Parade, Virginia Water, Surrey,
09904 4455.
Spogo, Format Ltd, Chobham Road, Sunningdale, Berkshire SL5 0DS;
0532 784211.
Stuburt Sports Footwear Ltd, Bridge Road, Kingswood, Bristol
BS15 4PP; *0272 568727.*
Stylo Matchmakers International Ltd, Clayton Wood Bank,
Leeds LS16 6RJ.

Publications

Magazines
Golf Weekly, Tallis House, Tallis Street, London EC4; *01-353 6000.*
Golf World, 41 Maltby Street, London SE1 3PA; *01-237 0043.*

Yearbooks
The Beacon Golfing Handbook, Beacon Publications, Jubilee House,
Billing Brook Road, Weston Favell, Northampton; *0604 487288.*
The Benson and Hedges Golfer's Handbook, Macmillan Publishers, Little
Essex Street, London WC2R 3LF; *01-836 6633.*
The Ebel World of Professional Golf, Springwood Books, 22 Chewter
Lane, Windlesham, Surrey GU22 6JP; *0276 74741.*